W9-BLF-993

## DATE DUE   19615

| MAR 1 7 2009 | | | |
|---|---|---|---|
| SEP 0 9 2008 | | | |
| SEP 27 2004 | | | |
| | | | |
| | | | |
| | | | |
| | | | |
| | | | |
| | | | |
| | | | |
| | | | |
| | | | |
| | | | |
| | | | |
| | | | |
| | | | |

Demco, Inc. 38-293

# Religion in Twentieth Century America

RELIGION
IN
AMERICAN
LIFE

**Religion in American Life**

JON BUTLER & HARRY S. STOUT
GENERAL EDITORS

# Religion in Twentieth Century America

*Randall Balmer*

OXFORD
UNIVERSITY PRESS

*For Christian, Andrew, and Sara*

## OXFORD
### UNIVERSITY PRESS

Oxford   New York
Athens   Auckland   Bangkok   Bogotá   Buenos Aires   Cape Town
Chennai   Dar es Salaam   Delhi   Florence   Hong Kong   Istanbul   Karachi
Kolkata   Kuala Lumpur   Madrid   Melbourne   Mexico City   Mumbai   Nairobi
Paris   São Paulo   Singapore   Taipei   Tokyo   Toronto   Warsaw
and associated companies in
Berlin   Ibadan

Copyright © 2001 by Randall Balmer
Published by Oxford University Press, Inc.
198 Madison Avenue, New York, New York 10016
www.oup.com

Oxford is a registered trademark of Oxford University Press

Library of Congress Cataloging-in-Publication Data

Balmer, Randall Herbert.
   Religion in twentieth century America / Randall Balmer.
      p. cm. - (Religion in American life)
   Includes bibliographical references and index.
   ISBN 0-19-511295-4 (library edition)
   1. United States-Religion-20th century. I. Title. II. Series.

BL2525.B35         2001
200'.973'0904-DC21    00-060674


9 8 7 6 5 4 3 2 1

Printed in the United States of America
on acid-free paper


Design and layout: Loraine Machlin
Picture research: Amla Sanghvi

*On the cover: Temples of God and Gold* by Frederick Detwiller.

*Frontispiece:* Celebrity panelists (from left) Ethel Waters, Herman Wouk, Grace Kelly, and
Charles E. Wilson appeared on the 1950s television program *Religion in American Life*. Many
Americans believed that church and synagogue attendance was a crucial weapon in the cold
war, and President Dwight Eisenhower encouraged it in this 1953 telecast.

# Contents

Editors' Introduction . . . . . . . . . . . . . . . . . . . . . . . . . . . . . . . . . . . .7
*Jon Butler and Harry S. Stout*

CHAPTER 1
Beginnings . . . . . . . . . . . . . . . . . . . . . . . . . . . . . . . . . . . . . . . . .11

CHAPTER 2
The Age of Militancy . . . . . . . . . . . . . . . . . . . . . . . . . . . . . . . . .25

CHAPTER 3
In God We Trust . . . . . . . . . . . . . . . . . . . . . . . . . . . . . . . . . . . .43

CHAPTER 4
Religion in the New Frontier . . . . . . . . . . . . . . . . . . . . . . . . . . .63

CHAPTER 5
Religion in an Age of Upheaval . . . . . . . . . . . . . . . . . . . . . . . . .83

CHAPTER 6
Preachers, Politicians, and Prodigals . . . . . . . . . . . . . . . . . . . . .99

CHAPTER 7
Religion for the New Millennium . . . . . . . . . . . . . . . . . . . . . . .113

Chronology . . . . . . . . . . . . . . . . . . . . . . . . . . . . . . . . . . . . . . .130

Further Reading . . . . . . . . . . . . . . . . . . . . . . . . . . . . . . . . . . . .134

Index . . . . . . . . . . . . . . . . . . . . . . . . . . . . . . . . . . . . . . . . . . . .139

# Editors' Introduction

JON BUTLER & HARRY S. STOUT, GENERAL EDITORS

n the 1960s, it was fashionable for theologians, public intellectuals, and academicians to proclaim the Death of God in the 20th century. They argued that the forces of modernization were so powerful that they would inevitably secularize western society and render religious belief old-fashioned. Churches and religious movements were doomed for extinction. But as *Religion in Twentieth Century America* makes clear, nothing could be further from the truth. Instead of dying, religion has thrived as never before. Whether measured by church attendance rates, national opinion polls, or charitable activities, this nation, arguably the most modern in the world, is also the most religious.

In this volume, Randall Balmer traces the steady growth of diverse religious groups from the dawn of the 20th century to its conclusion and a new millennium. Here the reader will encounter not only the large mainline Protestant denominations that shaped major institutions in America, but equally important, a host of vibrant, ever-growing "competitors" from Roman Catholics and Jews to pentecostals, Muslims, and a series of utopian and apocalyptic cults. Alongside the great religious movements and denominations, readers will also encounter religion in the marketplace, in politics, and in great events like World Wars I and II, the civil rights movement, and the formation of the Religious Right. Throughout the lesson is

Delegates from 34 Protestant denominations gathered in Philadelphia in 1908 to form the Federal Council of Churches of Christ, resolving "to manifest the essential oneness of the Christian Churches in America in Jesus Christ as their divine Lord and Savior."

unmistakable: for better and worse religion remained very much alive in the 20th century and showed no signs of extinction.

This book is part of a unique 17-volume series that explores the evolution, character, and dynamics of religion in American life from 1500 to the end of the 20th century. As late as the 1960s, historians paid relatively little attention to religion beyond studies of New England's Puritans. But since then, American religious history and its contemporary expression have been the subject of intense inquiry. These new studies have thoroughly transformed our knowledge of almost every American religious group and have fully revised our understanding of religion's role in U.S. history.

It is impossible to capture the flavor and character of the American experience without understanding the connections between secular activities and religion. Spirituality stood at the center of Native American societies before European colonization and has continued to do so long after. Religion—and the freedom to express it—motivated millions of immigrants to come to the United States from remarkably different cultures, and the exposure to new ideas and ways of living shaped their experience. It also fueled tension among different ethnic and racial groups in America and, regretfully, accounted for difficult episodes of bigotry in American society. Religion urged Americans to expand the nation—first within the continental United States, then through overseas conquests and missionary work—and has had a profound influence on American politics, from the era of the Puritans to the present. Finally, religion contributes to the extraordinary diversity that has, for four centuries, made the United States one of the world's most dynamic societies. The Religion in American Life series explores the historical traditions that have made religious freedom and spiritual exploration central features of American society. It emphasizes the experience of religion in America—what men and women have understood by religion, how it has affected politics and society, and how Americans have used it to shape their daily lives.

**Religion in American Life**

JON BUTLER & HARRY S. STOUT
**GENERAL EDITORS**

**RELIGION IN COLONIAL AMERICA**
*Jon Butler*

**RELIGION IN NINETEENTH CENTURY AMERICA**
*Grant Wacker*

**RELIGION IN TWENTIETH CENTURY AMERICA**
*Randall Balmer*

**BUDDHISTS, HINDUS, AND SIKHS IN AMERICA**
*Gurinder Singh Mann, Paul David Numrich & Raymond B. Williams*

**CATHOLICS IN AMERICA**
*James T. Fisher*

**JEWS IN AMERICA**
*Hasia R. Diner*

**MORMONS IN AMERICA**
*Claudia Lauper Bushman & Richard Lyman Bushman*

**MUSLIMS IN AMERICA**
*Frederick Denny*

**ORTHODOX CHRISTIANS IN AMERICA**
*John H. Erickson*

**PROTESTANTS IN AMERICA**
*Mark A. Noll*

**AFRICAN-AMERICAN RELIGION**
*Albert J. Raboteau*

**ALTERNATIVE AMERICAN RELIGIONS**
*Stephen J. Stein*

**CHURCH AND STATE IN AMERICA**
*Edwin S. Gaustad*

**IMMIGRATION AND AMERICAN RELIGION**
*Jenna Weissman Joselit*

**NATIVE AMERICAN RELIGION**
*Joel W. Martin*

**WOMEN AND AMERICAN RELIGION**
*Ann Braude*

**BIOGRAPHICAL SUPPLEMENT AND SERIES INDEX**
*Darryl Hart & Ann Henderson Hart*

## Chapter 1

# Beginnings

At the dawn of the 20th century the editor of a small magazine called the *Christian Oracle* thought that the turn of the calendar was so important that he would rename his publication *Christian Century*. "We believe that the coming century is to witness greater triumphs in Christianity than any previous century has ever witnessed," George A. Campbell, Jr., the editor, wrote from his Chicago office, "and that it is to be more truly Christian than any of its predecessors." The "Christian Century" that Campbell envisioned would be a *Protestant* century and, more specifically, a century defined by traditional, or "mainline," Protestant denominations—Presbyterian, Lutheran, Episcopalian, Methodist, Congregational, and Campbell's own Disciples of Christ.

Roman Catholics, however, had other ideas as they sought to make a place for themselves in the American religious landscape. In 1908 Pope Pius X declared that the United States was no longer a missionary territory for Roman Catholicism, meaning that the church in America was sufficiently well established that it required no further help from foreign Catholics. Later that same year, on November 16, American Catholics convened a missionary conference in Chicago to mark their passage from a church that *received* missionary help from others to a church that *sent* missionaries elsewhere. William H. O'Connell, archbishop of Chicago, noted the rapid maturity of the Roman Catholic Church in America. "It has covered the whole land of its birth and growth with its network of provinces and dioceses and parishes," he said, adding that American Catholicism had "taken on a character of its own; become conscious of its

Local organizers often had to construct special buildings such as the Scoville Tabernacle in Aurora, Missouri, in 1915, to hold the crowds attracted by early-20th-century itinerant preachers. Such gatherings often blended entertainment with religion.

own mission and destiny; and full of a strength and courage born of the air and free institutions of the name whence it derives its name, is prepared to go forth conquering and to conquer in the cause of Christ."

Indeed, Roman Catholics in America had withstood the 19th-century assaults of nativism, the organized attacks by Protestants and others who resented the arrival of Catholic and other non-Protestant immigrants. "The United States is Rome's favorite mission field," John L. Brandt had warned under the auspices of the American Protective Association as late as 1895, adding that "our country has been flooded with hordes of foreigners, many of whom are uneducated Roman Catholics, and who, from infancy, have yielded implicit obedience to the Pope." Within three years of the Chicago conference, however, the St. Mary's Mission House was established in Techny, Illinois, for the purpose of training and sending missionaries to other countries. In addition, two priests, Thomas F. Price and James A. Walsh, founded the Catholic Foreign Missionary Society of America in 1911. This society, located in Maryknoll, New York, dispatched missionaries throughout the world, especially to Latin America.

Other religious groups besides Catholics and more traditional Protestants staked their claim on the hearts and souls of Americans. On the first day of the new century, January 1, 1901, an event at Bethel Bible College in Topeka, Kansas, signaled a new era in American Protestantism. Agnes N. Ozman, a student at the school, began speaking in an unknown language, which some witnesses later identified as Chinese, despite the fact that Ozman had never studied the language. Students interpreted her ecstatic speech, which sounded like babbling, as a gift from the Holy Spirit, a phenomenon known as *glossolalia*, or "speaking in tongues." According to Christian doctrine, the first time that anyone had spoken in tongues had been recorded in the New Testament, in the second chapter of the Acts of the Apostles, when the Holy Spirit descended upon the early Christians on the feast of pentecost (so named because it occurred 50 days after Passover, the Jewish observance of the deliverance of ancient Israel from Egypt). On this occasion, after Jesus had been taken back into heaven, the Holy Spirit came upon the early believers "like a mighty wind," and they began speaking in unknown languages.

Although other incidents of *glossolalia* had been reported throughout church history—even Brigham Young, leader of the Mormons in the 19th century, claimed to have spoken in tongues—the small band of students at Bethel Bible College attached a special significance to the sudden reappearance of *glossolalia* on the opening day of the 20th century. The students believed that the spiritual gifts mentioned in the New Testament, which included divine healing of sickness or physical deformity as well as *glossolalia,* had been restored to the church in the last days before Jesus would return to Earth. This outpouring of the Holy Spirit would serve as the final wake-up call both for unbelievers and for those who claimed to be Christians but who had become spiritually indifferent. Through the actions of the Holy Spirit, this small band of students in Topeka believed, God was alive and well at the dawn of the 20th century, and God was issuing one final appeal before the end of time, just as the New Testament book of Revelation had predicted. These apocalyptic events, all promised in the book of Revelation, would engulf those who did not heed their urgent call to repentance.

According to pentecostal tradition, the modern movement began the day Agnes Ozman first spoke in tongues. The Assemblies of God ordained her in 1917. Ozman, shown here in a 1937 photograph, remained active in the movement throughout her life.

As the pentecostal revival spread among the students at Bethel Bible College, they were seized with a missionary zeal for bringing Christianity to America and to the world. These pentecostals, however, represented only one strain of evangelicalism in America, a movement characterized by a belief that the Bible should be interpreted literally and by its insistence on a conversion, or "born again," experience as the criterion for entering the kingdom of heaven. Pentecostals were distinct in that they added the Spiritual gifts, especially tongues and healing, to this definition of godliness. Agnes Ozman and other pentecostals craved religious emotions and feelings as a way to verify the presence of God in their lives.

From Topeka, pentecostalism spread rapidly. The founder of Bethel Bible College, Charles Fox Parham, had also spoken in tongues, which he interpreted as the "baptism of the Holy Spirit," an indication that God had especially blessed him and chosen him to proclaim the gospel. Parham was an itinerant preacher, and, following the New Year's Day revival in Topeka, he spread the word during his travels in Kansas, Missouri, and Texas. In Houston, Parham's message of Spirit baptism caught on with an African-American hotel waiter named William J. Seymour. A member of a group called the Evening Light Saints, Seymour carried the pentecostal message with him when he migrated west to Los Angeles in 1906. There, he conducted prayer meetings and soon began preaching to large audiences from the front porch of the house on Bonnie Brae Avenue, where he was staying. Soon the crowds, spilling onto the streets, became too unwieldy, and the gatherings moved to an abandoned warehouse at 312 Azusa Street.

The Azusa Street Revival, as the gathering came to be known, drew national and even worldwide attention to the new pentecostal movement. Meetings took place several times a day, and each lasted several hours. Participants sang hymns, listened to sermons, and heard testimonies from those who had been baptized by the Spirit, a scene reminiscent of the frontier camp meetings a century earlier. They raised their arms

Evangelist Pete Johnson preaches at Ferguson Alley in the Chinatown area of Los Angeles. As the world came to America in the form of immigrants, evangelicals in particular sought to convert them to Christianity.

toward heaven in a gesture of openness to the Holy Spirit, and they spoke in tongues. The San Francisco earthquake, which occurred just after five o'clock in the morning on April 18, 1906, added a new sense of urgency to the Azusa Street Revival. Did the catastrophe just a few hundred miles to the north portend the end of the world? Was Jesus coming right now?

Although the interpretations differed, participants were certain that God was at work on Azusa Street. Even more remarkable was that the revival was interracial—the "color line has been washed away by the blood" of Jesus, one participant exclaimed—and that women preached and spoke publicly about their faith in an age in which women were fighting even for the right to vote. The Azusa Street Revival spread its message through its own newspaper, the *Apostolic Faith,* and by means of itinerant preachers who fanned out across North America—to Chicago, Toronto, and other cities—bringing the pentecostal message of salvation and spiritual blessing. "Los Angeles Being Visited by a Revival of Bible Salvation and pentecost as Recorded in the Book of Acts," the *Apostolic Faith* proclaimed in its first issue, published in September 1906. "All over this city, God has been setting homes on fire and coming down and melting and saving and sanctifying and baptizing with the Holy Spirit," the newspaper continued, adding accounts of physical healings—of asthma, tuberculosis, even nearsightedness.

The *Apostolic Faith* also included news about a related phenomenon, called *xenolalia,* the gift of speaking a recognized language that the speaker had never before studied. "The Lord has given languages to the unlearned," the newspaper reported. "Greek, Latin, Hebrew, French, German, Italian, Chinese, Japanese, Zulu and languages of Africa, Hindu and Bengali and dialects of India, Chippewa and other languages of the Indians." Thus equipped and empowered by the Holy Spirit, missionaries left Los Angeles and carried news of the pentecostal revival across North America and throughout the world.

Even as missionaries from North America took their Christian message around the world, however, the world continued to come to the United States. Between 1900 and 1915, 15 million immigrants entered the country, most of them from southern or eastern Europe. In 1893, the

# The Azusa Street Revival in Los Angeles

*The first issue of the* Apostolic Faith, *newspaper of the Azusa Street Revival, was published in Los Angeles in September 1906, providing news about the extraordinary pentecostal revival taking place at 312 Azusa Street and elsewhere in the city. Many of the participants in the gatherings on Azusa Street spoke in tongues and claimed divine healing of sickness and physical deformity. This article appeared on the front page.*

PENTECOST HAS COME: LOS ANGELES BEING VISITED BY A REVIVAL OF BIBLE SALVATION AND PENTECOST AS RECORDED IN THE BOOK OF ACTS

The power of God now has this city agitated as never before. Pentecost has surely come and with it the Bible evidences are following, many being converted and sanctified and filled with the Holy Ghost, speaking in tongues as they did on the day of Pentecost. The scenes that are daily enacted in the building on Azusa Street and at Missions and churches in other parts of the city are beyond description, and the real revival is only started, as God has been working with His children mostly, getting them through to pentecost, and laying the foundation for a mighty wave of salvation among the unconverted.

World's Parliament of Religions, a gathering of representatives of the world's major religions, had convened in Chicago, meeting in the building that now houses the Art Institute of Chicago, on South Michigan Avenue. For the first time, Americans learned about traditions other than Christianity and Judaism. Swami Vivekananda, for example, made the case for Hinduism, Krishna, and Vedantic philosophy, which derives from the Vedas. These spiritual writings, he said, contained "the accumulated treasury of spiritual law discovered by different persons in different times." To a society still suffering the ravages of unbridled capitalism, the concentration of wealth in the hands of a very small number of people, Vivekananda declared: "It is good to love God for hope of reward in this or the next world, but it is better to love God for love's sake, and the prayer goes: 'Lord, I do not want wealth, nor children, nor learning.'" Following the World's Parliament, Vedanta societies sprouted up in the wake of Vivekananda's speaking tour throughout North America.

Anagarika Dharmapala of Ceylon (known today as Sri Lanka) introduced Americans to the "Middle Path" of Buddhism, the path between what he characterized as "the life of sensualism, which is low, ignoble, vulgar, unworthy and unprofitable," on the one hand, and "the pessimistic

Swami Vivekananda (wearing a turban) is surrounded by supporters at the Greenacre Religious Conference in Maine in 1894. After the World's Parliament of Religions, held in Chicago in 1893, Vivekananda traveled the country and organized Vedanta societies, dedicated to the advancement of Hinduism.

life of extreme asceticism," or self-denial, on the other. Buddhist beliefs and practices, which had already been present in Hawai'i and California in the 19th century—a Young Men's Buddhist Association was founded in Hawai'i in 1900, for instance—spread across the rest of North America. Mohammed Webb had the task of presenting Islam at the World's Parliament, asserting that Islam means "simply and literally resignation to the will of God." Like many of the representatives from other non-Christian religions, Webb lamented that most Americans had little understanding of religious traditions other than their own. As the 20th century unfolded, these religions—Hinduism, Buddhism, and Islam—along with many others, became increasingly common on the religious landscape of North America.

White Americans, however, had yet to make peace with those who had inhabited North America long before their arrival. Driven by the doctrine of "manifest destiny"—the notion that it was the destiny, even the responsibility, of the white man to seize control of the West from Native Americans—the United States government had engaged in an aggressive campaign of almost uninterrupted conquest throughout the latter half of the 19th century. (The only major setback occurred in 1876 when the Sioux defeated George Armstrong Custer and his troops at Little Big Horn, Montana, thereby embarrassing white Americans on the centennial of their Declaration of Independence.) Although attempts to Christianize Native Americans date back to the 16th century, the efforts had intensified during the 19th century as Methodists, Episcopalians, Baptists, Roman Catholics, Mennonites, and Presbyterians made a determined effort to convert the Sioux and Cherokees and Navajos and Pueblos to Christianity. Most resisted. "Christianity speaks of far-off lands and places," one observer noted, whereas Indian stories "tell of the four sacred mountains, at least one of which is visible almost everywhere in Navajo country."

In 1906 the United States government even sought to appropriate those mountains. When the U.S. Forest Service annexed vast tracts of Pueblo territory into the newly formed Kit Carson National Forest of northern New Mexico, the Pueblos objected to the inclusion of Taos Blue Lake, a sacred site, and they became especially alarmed when the Forest

Service began to cut trails and to allow grazing in the area. Although the 1848 Treaty of Guadalupe Hidalgo, which concluded the war with Mexico, had stipulated that the United States respect Spanish and Mexican land grants, a band of corrupt judges, lawyers, and territorial governors, known as the Santa Fe Ring, manipulated the bewildering court system to wrest lands from their rightful owners. Faced with the loss of Blue Lake, the Pueblos mounted vigorous protests; they staged demonstrations and wrote petitions, which argued for their religious freedoms based on the First Amendment to the Constitution and on the conviction that "the trees and all life and the earth itself . . . must be protected." "We have no buildings there, no steeples," Pueblo governor John C. Reyna noted. "There is nothing the human hand has made. The lake is our church. The mountain is our tabernacle. The evergreen trees are our living saints. . . . We pray to the water, the sun, the clouds, the sky, the deer. Without them we could not exist. They give us food, drink, physical power, knowledge."

Many Americans early in the 20th century, however, especially white Protestants, resented challenges to their status as the dominant religious

A nun teaches a class at St. Michael's School on the Navajo Reservation in Arizona around 1910. Although Rome once considered the United States a target for missionary activity, American Catholics themselves became increasingly active in missions after the turn of the 20th century.

group. Although Roman Catholics had been present in North America since the Spanish settlement of Florida and the Southwest and the French colonization of Quebec, Catholic immigrants from Germany and Italy were only beginning to acclimate themselves to the United States at the turn of the 20th century. Jews had been present in New Amsterdam (New York City) as early as 1654, but if they felt secure in a society that was still overwhelmingly Protestant, the execution of Leo Frank in 1915 jolted them out of their complacency.

Frank, a Jew born in Cuero, Texas, and reared in Brooklyn, New York, was plant superintendent of the National Pencil Company in Atlanta when Mary Phagan, a 14-year-old employee, was found murdered in the factory's basement on April 27, 1913. Frank was arrested the following day and charged with the crime. Even though the evidence was flimsy and the witnesses for the prosecution of dubious character, mobs inside and outside the courthouse demanded Frank's conviction. The jury obliged; he was convicted of the murder and sent to death row.

Simmering anti-Semitism, which had been implicit since Frank's arrest, boiled over during the appeals process. In the *Jeffersonian* magazine, Tom Watson, who later represented Georgia in the U.S. Senate, angrily demanded the execution of "the filthy, perverted Jew of New York." Watson also helped to form an anti-Semitic society, the Knights of Mary Phagan, which organized a boycott of Jewish stores and businesses throughout the state. After the U.S. Supreme Court turned down Frank's appeal, a last-minute reprieve from the governor of Georgia, John Slaton, commuted Frank's sentence to life in prison. Upon hearing the news, however, a mob stormed the state prison in Milledgeville, abducted the prisoner, transported him to Mary Phagan's hometown, and lynched him on August 16, 1915, while hurling anti-Semitic insults.

The Leo Frank case stunned and outraged Jews across the nation, prompting increased membership in such organizations as the Anti-Defamation League of B'nai B'rith (which means "sons of the covenant," a reference to ancient Israel) and sending southern Jews scurrying for refuge in northern cities. The cities remained a proving ground for ethnic, racial, and religious diversity at the turn of the 20th century. Several centuries earlier America's Protestants had envisioned a "city on a hill" and dreamed openly of establishing the kingdom of God in North America. By the close of the 19th century, however, so many "foreigners" had encroached upon that vision—Roman Catholics, Jews, African Americans, and even some practitioners of Eastern religions—that the squalid tenements on the lower east side of Manhattan, for instance, no longer resembled the kingdom of God.

"Where God builds a church the devil builds next door a saloon, is an old saying that has lost its point in New York," the social reformer Jacob Riis wrote in *How the Other Half Lives* in 1890. "Either the devil was on the ground first, or he has been doing a good deal more in the way of building. I tried once to find out how the account stood, and counted to 111 Protestant churches, chapels and places of worship of every kind below Fourteenth Street, 4,065 saloons. The worst half of the tenement population lives down there, and it has to this day the worst half of the saloons. Uptown the account stands a little better, but there are easily ten saloons to every church to-day. I am afraid, too, that the congregations are larger by a good deal; certainly the attendance is steadier and the contributions more liberal the week round, Sunday included."

America's Protestants were divided on their approach to the cities and to the social problems they presented. Many of the more conservative Protestants, known as evangelicals, who had condemned Charles Darwin's theory of evolution and who, in response to attacks on the Bible, had formulated a doctrine insisting that the Bible contained absolutely no errors or contradictions, grew increasingly suspicious of the cities, seeing

The 1915 lynching of Leo Frank by an anti-Semitic vigilante mob in Georgia sent shock waves through the American Jewish community, especially in the South. Frank had been elected president of the local chapter of the Anti-Defamation League of B'nai B'rith in 1912.

them as seedbeds of sin and dens of political corruption. In 1892, for example, Charles H. Parkhurst, pastor of the Madison Park Presbyterian Church in New York City, had criticized the corrupt politicians in city hall as a "lying, perjured, rum-soaked" lot and decried "the official and administrative criminality that is filthifying our entire municipal life, making New York a very hotbed of knavery, debauchery and bestiality."

Massive changes in American society following the Civil War, especially the rise of industry and the growth of the cities, had prompted evangelicals to revise their expectations that Jesus would return to Earth after they had built the kingdom of God. Although such organizations as the Young Men's Christian Association (YMCA), the Young Women's Christian Association (YWCA), and the Salvation Army made valiant efforts to sanitize the squalor and to rein in the rowdiness of urban life, and Carry A. Nation, a vigorous opponent of alcohol, had wielded her hatchet against the "hell holes" and "murder mills" of saloons, most evangelicals had succumbed to despair about the mess they saw everywhere around them. They revised their theology, insisting, contrary to the beliefs animating evangelicals earlier in the 19th century, that the world would *not* improve before Jesus came back to Earth. "I view this world as a wrecked vessel," Dwight L. Moody, a Chicago preacher, declared. "The Lord has given me a lifeboat and said, 'Moody, save all you can.'" In this new formulation, known as dispensationalism because it divides all of human history into ages, or time periods (dispensations), Jesus would return at any moment. History would come screeching to a halt, and the predictions contained in the book of Revelation would then unfold.

Dispensationalism, this revised interpretation concerning the end of time, may look harmless enough at first glance. It represented a way for America's evangelicals, at one time the majority religious group in North America, to reassert their importance. They might no longer dominate American society in the way they did before the Civil War, but this new interpretation of Revelation provided them the assurance that they understood the mind of God. They had figured it out, they had cracked the code, and they knew exactly how history would end. More important, however, dispensationalism exempted them from the daunting task of social reform. What was the use of reforming society according to the standards of godliness? Jesus would return at any moment, summon the "true believers" (the evangelicals), and unleash judgment against those who had opposed them. Dispensationalism, this "theology of despair," allowed evangelicals to walk away from the problems of the cities and to concentrate on the conversion, or regeneration, of individuals rather than society as a whole.

Not all Protestants followed this model. A large number, who were generally regarded as more liberal, theologically and politically, insisted that the gospel of the New Testament was capable not only of saving sinful individuals but of transforming sinful social institutions as well. The Christian gospel "has its ministry of rescue and healing for sinning men and women," Henry Sloane Coffin, a Protestant theologian, acknowledged, but it also "has its plan of spiritual health for society." These liberal Protestants, led by such pastors as Walter Rauschenbusch, Washington Gladden, and others, preached the Social Gospel, which held that Christians had a responsibility to reform abuses in the workplace, in the marketplace, and in the political arena. "No plan can be devised which will give us good city government," Gladden wrote in 1909, "so long as the great majority of our citizens are unwilling to take any responsibility for the government of our cities."

Whereas evangelicals had retreated to dispensationalism, believing that the evils of society stemmed from sinful individuals in need of redemption, those who promoted the Social Gospel believed that human nature was essentially good and that goodness had been thwarted by corrupt institutions. By the middle of the 1910s, however, that assumption of innate human goodness would be severely tested by the winds of war already gusting in Europe.

EXIT

## Chapter 2

# The Age of Militancy

Many religious leaders opposed the entry of the United States into World War I (known then as the "Great War"). Peace advocates included Henry Sloane Coffin, a theologically liberal professor at Union Theological Seminary in New York City, and the three-time Democratic candidate for President, William Jennings Bryan, who was theologically conservative and politically liberal. Bryan served as secretary of state under Woodrow Wilson until 1915, when he resigned rather than take steps toward war. By early 1917, however, popular sentiments had changed.

"It is a terrible thing to lead this great and peaceful people into war," Wilson acknowledged in his war message to Congress, but Americans responded to Wilson's summons to "make the world safe for democracy." By and large only such long-standing pacifists as the Quakers and the Mennonites opposed the war, and the language of Christianity became the religion of American patriotism. Billy Sunday, for example, a flamboyant revivalist and former baseball player, conducted "hang the kaiser" rallies. "Christianity and Patriotism are synonymous terms," he declared, "and hell and traitors are synonymous."

Divisions between liberal and conservative Protestants hardened in the early decades of the 20th century. The two camps had differed over their approach to the cities—liberal advocates of the Social Gospel had urged the redemption of sinful social institutions, whereas conservatives focused increasingly on the salvation of individuals—but liberals, known

An eager crowd awaits the arrival of Billy Sunday at New York City's Pennsylvania Station. With impressive advance work and the antics of a showman, Sunday, a former baseball player who converted to evangelical Christianity, helped to bring revival preaching to the cities.

# The Evils of War

*The Protestant magazine* Christian Century *was founded as the* Christian Oracle *in 1884 and renamed at the turn of the 20th century. Although the editors of the* Christian Century, *like many Americans, had initially been opposed to the entry of the United States into World War I, the magazine came to recognize the perils of German aggression. In this editorial, "The War and the Social Gospel," which appeared in the December 27, 1917, issue, the magazine used the occasion of armed conflict to meditate on the theological problem of evil, both personal and corporate.*

Even in the war itself, in its inherent character, we have the illumination of a great social principle which has a vital bearing on our theology of sin. Too long have we thought of sin in its personal and individual embodiment alone. A great hindrance in the way of realizing Christ's social gospel of the Kingdom of God has been the fact that we have been unable to recognize sin in its collective or social embodiment. . . . The sin we are fighting is not that of the individual German soldier through whose breasts our boys have to run their bayonets, but the social sin of the German nation as a whole. . . . With the mind of the world grown accustomed to think of Germany as a "super-personal" force of evil, it will be incomparably easier to apply the principle of social sinning to groups and institutions within a single nation and to bring to bear upon them through the social gospel the super-personal forces of condemnation and destruction.

also as "modernists," generally sought to reconcile the gospel with the modern world. Darwin's theory of evolution, they argued, was not inconsistent with Christian faith; believers simply must shed their antiquated insistence on interpreting the Genesis account of creation literally. Human nature, they said, was basically good and altruistic, a notion that seemed to be contradicted by the war in Europe.

Conservatives, also known as evangelicals, came increasingly to distrust the modernists and the theological liberalism that evangelicals believed was steadily infecting Protestant denominations. In an effort to stanch the spread of modernist ideas, Lyman and Milton Stewart, founders of Union Oil Company in California, established a fund of a quarter-million dollars to publish and distribute a series of booklets "to every pastor, evangelist, minister, theology professor, theological student, Sunday school superintendent, YMCA and YWCA secretary in the English-speaking world." These twelve booklets appeared between 1910 and 1915 and were known collectively as *The Fundamentals.*

Subtitled *A Testimony to the Truth,* the series of booklets contained conservative theological statements written by prominent evangelical theologians from Great Britain, Canada, and the United States. The articles defended such doctrines as biblical inerrancy (the idea that the Bible was completely free from error in the original manuscripts), the Virgin Birth of Christ (that Jesus was born of the Virgin Mary), the authenticity of miracles (that the miracles attributed to Jesus took place exactly as recorded in the New Testament), and the Genesis account of creation. Those who subscribed to these doctrines came to be known as "fundamentalists." *The Fundamentals* served as a rallying cry for conservatives in their battle against modernism.

On May 21, 1922, one of the most articulate and influential liberal preachers in America, Harry Emerson Fosdick, laid down the gauntlet in his historic sermon, "Shall the Fundamentalists Win?" "Already all of us must have heard about the people who call themselves the Fundamentalists," Fosdick told his congregation at the First Presbyterian Church in New York City. "Their apparent intention is to drive out of the evangelical churches men and women of liberal opinions." The venerable preacher proceeded to characterize fundamentalists as opposed to modern learning and poised to overtake American Protestantism. "In such an hour, delicate and dangerous, when feelings are bound to run high," he intoned, "I plead this morning the cause of magnanimity and liberality and tolerance of spirit." Fosdick concluded that the fundamentalists would never succeed in their effort "to drive out from the Christian churches all the consecrated souls who do not agree with their theory of inspiration."

Indeed, by the mid-1920s it appeared that the modernists had gained the upper hand, at least in their struggle to control the denominations. Fundamentalist forces among Baptists in the North decried the liberalism at the University of Chicago Divinity School and formed their own school in Chicago, Northern Baptist Theological Seminary, in 1913. Among Presbyterians, J. Gresham Machen, a professor at the denomination's Princeton Theological Seminary, published *Christianity and Liberalism* in 1923, arguing that liberal theology was, in fact, a new religion. It was *not* Christianity, he insisted, and liberals should do the honorable thing and leave the denomination.

The liberals, or modernists, would do no such thing. In 1924, when the Presbyterian general assembly adopted a measure that allowed clergy to restate historic doctrines in their own words, conservatives bewailed the move as a slippery slope into theological error. By 1929 Machen left his post at Princeton Seminary to form, successively, Westminister Theological Seminary in Philadelphia, a foreign missions board independent of the denomination, and the Presbyterian Church of America, later known as the Orthodox Presbyterian Church—all dedicated to conservative theology.

Fundamentalists defected from other denominations as well, seeking to separate themselves from what they regarded as heresy, a departure from traditional Christian doctrines. They embarked on an ambitious program of forming their own congregations, denominations, mission societies, publishing houses, colleges, seminaries, and Bible institutes—all of them free from the taint of modernism. This sprawling network of institutions throughout the United States and Canada would comprise an evangelical subculture, which provided the foundation for the return of evangelicals to political activism in the 1970s.

The fundamentalist-modernist controversies of the 1920s, the fights between conservatives and liberals, were often highly pitched battles, but the most famous skirmish of all took place on the second story of the Rhea County courthouse in Dayton, Tennessee. The state of Tennessee had passed the Butler Act, which prohibited, in the law's words, "the teaching of the evolutionary theory in all the universities, normals, and all the public schools of Tennessee." Almost immediately, the American Civil Liberties Union (ACLU) advertised that it was looking for someone to challenge the law, and on May 4, 1925, a group of civic boosters gathered at Fred Robinson's drugstore in Dayton and plotted a court case that would put the town on the map. They summoned the local high school's general science instructor and part-time football coach, plied him with a fountain drink, and asked if he would be willing to test the Butler Act. The teacher, John T. Scopes, it turned out, could not recall whether or not he had actually taught evolution, but that detail seemed irrelevant to everyone concerned. Scopes agreed to challenge the case, whereupon the local law-enforcement officer served him with a warrant, and Scopes left the drugstore to play a game of tennis.

A much larger drama was being played out, of course, and the 24-year-old teacher was lost in the shuffle. The ACLU retained the services of renowned trial lawyer Clarence Darrow as head of Scopes's defense team, while William Jennings Bryan, a stem-winding orator, assisted the prosecution. "We have the purpose of preventing bigots and ignoramuses from controlling the education of the United States," Darrow declared, "and that is all." Bryan saw the trial differently, as a test of whether taxpayers could determine what their children were taught. Bryan also harbored serious misgivings about the social effects of evolutionary theory, fearing that the survival-of-the-fittest doctrine could be used to justify the ravages of military force, territorial conquest, and the unbridled pursuit of wealth. As early as 1904 he had denounced Darwinism "because it represents man as reaching his present perfection by the operation of the law of hate—the merciless law by which the strong crowd out and kill the weak."

Surrounded by spectators with rolled-up shirtsleeves in a steamy, second-story courtroom in Dayton, Tennessee, two old friends, Clarence Darrow (standing) and William Jennings Bryan (holding a fan), squared off on opposite sides. Darrow defended John T. Scopes, a local school teacher accused of violating the state's Butler Act, which forbade the teaching of evolution in public schools.

For 10 sweltering days in July 1925 the Scopes trial unfolded amid a carnival atmosphere. Partisans from both sides squared off on the court-house lawn; vendors sold souvenirs emblazoned with the likenesses of monkeys, a reference to the theory that humans evolved from apes. The media contingent, headed by H. L. Mencken of the *Baltimore Sun*, had arrived in full force, and the proceedings were broadcast live over radio station WGN in Chicago.

Whereas Darrow appealed to the "intelligent, scholarly Christians, who by the millions in the United States find no inconsistency between evolu-tion and religion," Bryan sought to cast the issue in different terms: "Can a minority in this State come in and compel a teacher to teach that the Bible is not true and make the parents of these children pay the expenses of the teacher to tell their children what these people believe is false and danger-ous?" The turning point of the trial occurred when Darrow persuaded

Bryan to take the witness stand. In so doing, they flip-flopped the roles of prosecutor and defendant because Darrow, counsel for the defense, thrust Bryan into the role of defending the truth of the Bible. Darrow succeeded in making Bryan look foolish, especially as the trial was reported by Mencken, who was Darrow's close friend. Mencken relegated Bryan and fundamentalists to the "mean streets" of America, "everywhere where learning is too heavy a burden for mortal minds to carry."

A point nearly lost amid the overheated rhetoric from the overheated courtroom in Dayton was that Scopes was in fact found guilty of violating the Butler Act and fined $100, although the conviction was later overturned by the Tennessee Supreme Court on a technicality. Bryan and the fundamentalists lost in the larger courtroom of public opinion, however, just five years after one of their biggest triumphs—the enactment of the Eighteenth Amendment to the U.S. Constitution, prohibiting the sale and consumption of alcohol.

Bryan died five days after the conclusion of the trial, and in the years following the "Scopes monkey trial" fundamentalists continued their wholesale retreat from the broader American society, which they regarded as both corrupt and corrupting. For half a century after the trial—from 1925 until about 1975, with the Presidential campaign of Jimmy Carter, a Southern Baptist Sunday school teacher—fundamentalists rarely ventured outside of the evangelical subculture. They remained content within their private world of churches, denominations, schools, Bible camps, and mission societies. Many even refused to vote, so convinced were they of the corruptions of the world outside their subculture.

The modernists, by all appearances, had prevailed in the fundamentalist-modernist battles during the 1920s. By absenting themselves from the denominations in large numbers, the conservatives had ceded Protestant denominations to the liberals. The spoils of victory included everything from church buildings and denominational offices to pension funds and seminary scholarships. While the fundamentalists had to start from scratch, the modernists sought to consolidate their positions. In 1925 the Presbyterians, the Methodists, and the Congregationalists in Canada merged to form the United Church of Canada. To the south, the Federal

An Ohio chapter of the Knights of Columbus, around 1914. Especially during the World Wars, the Knights emphasized their allegiance to both Catholic church and country.

Council of Churches, which had been organized in 1908, continued to pursue the agenda, in the words of Charles S. Macfarland, the council's general secretary, of "modern movements towards Christian unity."

American Catholics also recognized the virtues of consolidation and cooperation. The Knights of Columbus, an organization for Catholic laymen, had been formed in 1882 to provide insurance and to offer recreational and social opportunities in the days before mass entertainment. During World War I, the Knights successfully petitioned the government to allow Catholic soldiers to use the Knights of Columbus as their service organization rather than the Protestant YMCA. The National Catholic War Council, which had been formed in 1917 to recruit and train military chaplains, took the name National Catholic Welfare Conference after the war. The organization, which provided the opportunity for Catholic bishops to speak with a united voice, set up offices in Washington, where they sought to influence public policy on issues relating to Roman Catholicism.

Perhaps the most important organizational efforts of the Roman Catholic Church were directed toward youth. In 1884, at a national gathering in Baltimore known as the Third Plenary Council, Catholic leaders had sought to address the perils of rearing Catholic children in an overwhelmingly Protestant culture. The bishops' battles against Protestant

biases in public schools had triggered "great school wars" in New York, Philadelphia, and others cities, but despite, for instance, Catholic objections to the use of the Protestant King James Version of the Bible, little had changed.

The Third Plenary Council directed that all Catholic parishes set up parochial (parish) schools or otherwise provide for Catholic children's upbringing in the faith. By the early decades of the 20th century parochial schools had been established throughout the country in an effort to ensure that Catholic schoolchildren remained Catholic. In addition, the church had other strategies for appealing to younger Catholics and keeping them within the fold. The Catholic Youth Organization (CYO) was founded by a Chicago priest, Bernard J. Shiel, in 1930 to provide recreational activities for Catholics and an alternative to the Protestant-dominated YMCA and YWCA. Chapters of the CYO, which sponsored basketball leagues, boxing tournaments, and other athletic events, flourished around the country.

American Jews also began to organize in the early decades of the 20th century. On November 9, 1926, a gathering of Jewish leaders in New York City led to the formation of the Synagogue Council of America, based on the assumption that "it is desirable that the representatives of the synagogues in America meet from time to time in order to take counsel

together for the sacred purpose of preserving and fostering Judaism."
Conservative Judaism saw itself as a middle ground between the Orthodox, or strictly observant, Jews who had recently arrived from Eastern
Europe, and Reform Judaism, which had so assimilated to America that
many Reform Jewish congregations had replaced Hebrew with English in
the prayer book and had given up both the segregation of men from
women during worship and the observance of Kosher dietary laws.

Just as the American context has given rise to a variety of religious
expressions, so, too, Judaism in America has taken a number of different
forms. In 1922 Mordecai M. Kaplan, a rabbi and a professor at the Jewish
Theological Seminary, assumed leadership of the Society for the
Advancement of Judaism in New York City and opened a "Jewish Center"
on Manhattan's West Side, a combination of synagogue, assembly hall,
gymnasium, and classrooms. The Jewish Center reflected Kaplan's vision
of religion serving the social needs of a minority culture. Judaism, he
insisted, was the folk religion of the Jewish people, and it was no longer
necessary to believe in an otherworldly, personal God. Instead, as Kaplan
argued in *Judaism as a Civilization,* published in 1934, Jews should
"reconstruct" their lives around Jewish culture. The movement Kaplan
inspired, called Reconstructionism, assured Jews that religious obser-
vances were important only insofar as they reminded them of their history and culture, and Kaplan called on Jews to unite behind their common
ethnic and cultural identity.

Other Americans consolidated as well. "America for Americans,"
Hiram Wesley Evans, who billed himself as "Imperial Wizard and Emper-
or, Knights of the Ku Klux Klan," declared amid a resurgence of Klan
activity in the 1920s. The Ku Klux Klan, or KKK, a secretive organization
of white supremacists, had been founded in Nashville after the Civil War
and then revived as a Protestant lodge by a former Methodist minister,
William J. Simmons, in 1915. Evans and others were attracted to the Klan's
intolerance for Jews, Catholics, and African Americans. "The white race
must be supreme, not only in America but in the world," Evans declared.
"Protestantism is an essential part of Americanism; without it America
could never have been created and without it she cannot go forward."

Prejudice against Roman Catholics persisted to the north as well. In late 1922 and early 1923, 16 large Catholic churches in Quebec caught fire under mysterious circumstances, and the three oldest shrines in the province were destroyed by fire—the Trappist monastery at Oka; Sainte Anne de Beaupré, noted for its miraculous cures; and the Basilica in Quebec City, which had been built in 1647.

After the turn of the 20th century the lynching of African Americans became frightfully commonplace, especially in the South. Reconstruction, the plan to rebuild the South after the Civil War, had failed to provide equality of opportunity across racial lines. In addition, the emergence of the so-called Jim Crow laws, which segregated whites and blacks, and the spread of the boll weevil, which caused cotton crop failures, all prompted many African Americans to leave the South and migrate to northern cities, bringing with them a rich cultural heritage. The musical tradition of the blues, for example, can be traced from the Delta region in Mississippi, north to Beale Street in Memphis, to Kansas City and St. Louis, and finally to the South Side of Chicago.

African American migrations tended to follow the train lines, which ran south and north, and so blacks from Georgia and the Carolinas ended up in Washington or Newark or New York City, whereas blacks from

Two hooded KKK pilots pose next to an airplane in Dayton, Ohio, in 1924. In the 1920s, Klan members were increasingly brazen with their demonstrations against Catholics, Jews, and African Americans.

CONVENTION ADDRESS
BY
HON. MARCUS GARVEY
DELIVERING CONSTITUTION
FOR
NEGRO RIGHTS

LIBERTY HALL

In 1920 Marcus Garvey, founder of the Universal Negro Improvement Association, presided over an international gathering of black people. The convention, held in New York City, issued a Constitution for Negro Rights, which called for freedom from white domination in Africa.

Alabama and Mississippi settled in Cleveland or Chicago. Their religious beliefs and practices found new expressions in an urban setting. Many African Americans, seeking to replicate the close-knit communities of the South, found a spiritual home in storefront churches, where worhip was marked by enthusiasm and ecstasy. Others sought the middle-class respectability of the Baptists or the African Methodist Episcopal churches. Still others gravitated toward a new generation of religious leaders—Father Divine or Marcus Garvey or Daddy Grace or Timothy Drew.

Garvey, a native of Jamaica who came to the United States in 1916, preached that God was black, and taught the gospel of black superiority and unity. He rallied his followers under the banner of the Universal Negro Improvement Association. The slogan for Garvey's movement was "One God! One Aim! One Destiny!" and he formed a steamship company, the Black Star Line, in order to resettle African Americans in Africa. The venture soon attracted the scrutiny of federal authorities, however; Garvey was convicted of mail fraud in 1925 and thrown into prison. Calvin Coolidge commuted his sentence in 1927, and Garvey eventually died in London in 1940. Despite Garvey's demise, other African Americans found his message of black pride irresistible. Timothy Drew, who became known as the Noble Drew Ali, insisted that the true religion of blacks was Islam, and his Moorish Science Temple, begun in Newark, New Jersey, in 1913, told blacks of their "true heritage" as Moorish Americans. Although Ali disappeared under mysterious circumstances in 1929, his message of black identity and pride would be picked up later by the Nation of Islam.

Other African-American religious leaders echoed the message of racial pride and uplift, especially during the heady days of the Harlem

Renaissance, a flowering of black culture and the arts during the 1920s. One of the more riveting figures of this era was Major Jealous Divine, known to his followers as Father Divine. He operated a boardinghouse and an employment bureau in Sayville, Long Island, New York. Divine's lavish, sometimes raucous, celebrations, which in the theology of his Peace Mission Movement held religious significance, offended some of the Sayville neighbors, especially those who objected to the interracial nature of the gatherings. In 1931 Divine was arrested for disturbing the peace. He stood trial in the courtroom of Judge Lewis J. Smith, whose comportment betrayed his prejudice against African Americans. The jury returned a verdict of guilty but urged leniency in sentencing. The judge, however, imposed the maximum sentence and sent Divine to jail. Three days later Smith, who had apparently been in good health, died suddenly.

When informed of the judge's demise, Father Divine, who had never discouraged speculation among his followers that he possessed supernatural powers, responded with one of the most unforgettable lines in all of American religious history: "I hated to do it." Divine was released from jail shortly thereafter.

Although American soldiers had returned triumphant from Europe at the conclusion of the "Great War," having made "the world safe for democracy," it was clear that the United States still had much work to do at home to ensure freedom and equality for its own citizens. The Presidential election of 1928 demonstrated the persistence of anti-Catholic bias among the nation's Protestants. Alfred E. Smith, governor of New York and the Democratic nominee for President, faced relentless attacks because he was Roman Catholic, a fact that led some Protestant groups to oppose him outright. More often, however, Smith's detractors shrouded their anti-Catholicism behind rhetoric about the candidate's opposition to Prohibition and his support for repeal of the Eighteenth Amendment.

"I do not wish any member of my faith in any part of the United States to vote for me on any religious grounds," Smith declared during the campaign. "I want them to vote for me only when in their hearts and consciences they become convinced that my election will promote the best interests of our country." In part because of his faith, however,

Smith lost the general election to Herbert C. Hoover, a Republican from West Branch, Iowa, in Hoover's first bid for elective office. (According to popular lore at the time, when Smith lost the election he sent a one-word telegram to the pope: "Unpack.") The Eighteenth Amendment and the republic itself, in the eyes of many Protestants, had been rescued from the threats of "Rum and Romanism," a reference to the Roman Catholic Church.

Hoover's triumph was short-lived. On "Black Thursday," October 24, 1929, less than eight months after he took office, the stock market collapsed and plunged the nation into the depths of the Great Depression. The new President was temperamentally incapable of the dramatic action needed to pull the nation out of its economic crisis, so when he faced another governor of New York, Franklin Delano Roosevelt, in the 1932 election, the results were different. Although Roosevelt had campaigned against any extraordinary governmental interference in the workings of the economy, his attitude had changed by the time of his inauguration. Roosevelt's New Deal offered wildly experimental approaches to economic renewal, an "alphabet soup" of federal agencies that would attack the root causes of the collapse and put Americans back to work.

Arguing that the only thing Americans need fear was "fear itself," Roosevelt took to the radio to provide comfort and assurance in his "fireside chats." In so doing he was using for political ends a medium already used to considerable effect by religious leaders. In 1922 a pentecostal preacher named Aimee Semple McPherson became the first woman ever to preach a sermon over the radio, and her station, KFSG ("Kalling Four Square Gospel") was the nation's first station owned and operated by a religious organization. "Sister Aimee," as she was known, built her spectacular Angelus Temple in the Echo Park

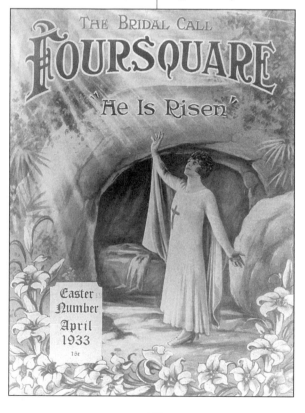

In this dramatic 1933 magazine cover, Aimee Semple McPherson tried to compete with Hollywood, across town from her Angelus Temple in the Echo Park neighborhood of Los Angeles. "Sister Aimee" overcame a poor childhood and the death of her first husband to become one of the most colorful religious figures in American history.

neighborhood of Los Angeles in 1923. That same year Charles E. Fuller began broadcasting his *Old Fashioned Revival Hour,* a mix of music and evangelical preaching. By the 1940s Fuller's weekly broadcast from the Long Beach Auditorium would be the most popular radio program in the country, eclipsing Amos 'n' Andy, Bob Hope, and Charlie McCarthy.

Not all religious radio broadcasters were Protestants. Charles E. Coughlin, a Roman Catholic priest from Royal Oak, Michigan, took to the radio airwaves in 1926 with the idea of explaining Catholicism to America's Protestants after the Ku Klux Klan had burned a cross at his Shrine of the Little Flower. Coughlin, who counted the automobile manufacturer Henry Ford among his friends, quickly expanded his purview to politics, sounding themes calculated to appeal to the masses. He established his National Union for Social Justice in 1934 and argued that "the old economic system of ragged, rugged individualism was nurtured at the twin breasts of successive Republican and Democratic Administrations—the right breast exuding the sour milk" of wealth and privilege and the left breast the "skimmed milk" of socialism. Although Coughlin had initially supported Roosevelt's New Deal, the "radio priest" eventually

Charles E. Fuller (far left) shares the stage with his wife, Grace Payton Fuller (right), a choir, and a gospel quartet. His weekly radio show *Old Fashioned Revival Hour,* broadcast live from the Long Beach Auditorium in southern California, attracted millions of listeners with its blend of lively singing and homespun preaching.

turned against it, railing against the President and engaging in anti-Semitic and pro-Nazi rhetoric until the Catholic bishops forced him off the air in 1940.

Despite Roosevelt's best efforts, however, economic recovery proved elusive throughout the 1930s, giving rise to demagogues, religious and otherwise. The resurgent Ku Klux Klan directed some of its hatred toward Jews, in addition to its more traditional targets, blacks and Roman Catholics. Gerald Burton Winrod, head of an organization called Defenders of the Christian Faith, based in Topeka, Kansas, railed against modernism in its various forms, including Darwinism, the New Deal, Communism, and what he believed was a worldwide Jewish conspiracy. Winrod's conspiracy theories anticipated some of the white supremacist rhetoric of various so-called Christian Identity movements in the 1980s and 1990s.

Not all of the religious rhetoric during the Depression, however, was hateful. On May 1, 1933, Dorothy Day and Peter Maurin began distributing the *Catholic Worker* in New York City's Union Square. The small newspaper, published out of a dwelling on the lower East Side of Manhattan, sold for a penny a copy, and it provided Roman Catholic social teaching regarding the poor and the unemployed. The cure for the ills of society, the newspaper declared, lay in a return to such radical Christian values as pacifism and concern for the less fortunate, including workers. Following Day's example, those associated with the Catholic Worker Movement lived in "voluntary poverty" and directed their energies toward people on the margins of society. Catholic Worker houses expanded to other cities, and the movement retained its opposition to the military through World War II and the Korean and Vietnam Wars.

The years surrounding World War I and the Great Depression called traditional religious beliefs into question. Modernists cast off the moorings of creeds and biblical literalism. Fundamentalists came to regard science, especially Darwinism, as a threat, rather than an ally. Americans' faith in unfettered capitalism was sorely tested by the stock market crash of 1929, and that same year a young newly appointed professor at Union Theological Seminary in New York City, Reinhold Niebuhr, called liberal

In the office of the *Catholic Worker,* Dorothy Day (seated at right) and her colleagues work on a 1934 issue of the newspaper, which sold for a penny.

theology into question. Ever since the 19th century, theological liberals had asserted the essential goodness of humanity and had sought to reconcile the gospel of the New Testament with the modern world. They played down the notion of human sinfulness, argued that human nature was basically good and altruistic, and identified the kingdom of God with social progress.

For Niebuhr and other advocates of a theology that became known as Neo-Orthodoxy in a reference to their attempt to recover some traditional elements of Protestant theology, the ravages of World War I and the devastation of the Great Depression had shattered the liberals' naive belief in the goodness of the human nature. Drawing in part on the writings of Karl Barth, a Protestant theologian from Switzerland, Niebuhr reintroduced the Christian doctrine of original sin, which explained the presence of evil in the world. What Niebuhr called the "political realism of Christian orthodoxy" took full account of evil and endorsed "the coercive force of governments to restrain those who will not voluntarily abide by the rule of rational justice." Although Niebuhr's Neo-Orthodoxy, also known as the theology of crisis, drew criticism from both the liberals and the evangelicals, its assertion of human depravity and its justification of force to restrain evil became especially prophetic as the world drifted once again toward war.

## Chapter 3

# In God We Trust

"Our form of government makes no sense unless it is founded in a deeply felt religious faith," President Dwight Eisenhower declared in 1952, "and I don't care what it is." By the middle decades of the 20th century Americans were growing increasingly confused and uneasy about the varieties of religion around them. The days when Protestants dominated American society, as they had in the 19th century, were fading fast. Protestants had to make room for others, especially Catholics and Jews, who had taken advantage of the Statue of Liberty's famous invitation: "Give me your tired, your poor, your huddled masses yearning to breathe free."

American Protestants not only had to deal with the presence of Jews, Catholics, and others within the United States, they also had to reconsider their attitudes toward those of different faiths throughout the world. Although the missionary impulse had been strong in the 19th century (and it continued throughout the 20th), some Protestants began to assess the entire missionary enterprise. In 1930 an organization called the Laymen's Foreign Missions Inquiry, with the support of seven Protestant denominations and the financial backing of the oil tycoon John D. Rockefeller, Jr., undertook a study of Protestant foreign missions. The organization sent delegates to interview missionaries in several countries throughout the world and then entrusted the findings to a commission chaired by William Ernest Hocking, professor of philosophy at Harvard University.

The Hocking commission issued a seven-volume appraisal of Protestant missions, together with detailed recommendations. The commission's report, and especially its one-volume summary entitled *Re-Thinking Missions,* heralded a new era in missionary work, calling for American Protestants to be more sensitive to other cultures and other religions. "There is a growing conviction that the mission enterprise is at a fork in the road," the report began, "and that momentous decisions are called for." *Re-Thinking Missions* argued for greater respect for the integrity of other religions, questioned the quality of missionaries in the field, and urged that "a much more critical selection of candidates should be made, even at the risk of curtailing the number of missionaries sent out."

Pearl S. Buck, a Presbyterian and the wife of a missionary to China, reviewed *Re-Thinking Missions* in the Protestant magazine *Christian Century.* Buck, whose novel *The Good Earth* won the Pulitzer Prize in 1932, the same year that the Hocking Report appeared, hailed *Re-Thinking Missions* as "inspired" and "a masterpiece of constructive religious thought." Other, more conservative Protestants were not so impressed, seeing the Hocking Report as yet another example of how liberals were backing away from truth and certainty, allowing themselves to be swallowed into the quicksand of theological relativism, where any other religion might be just as valid as Christianity.

While evangelicals and fundamentalists tried to walk the straight and narrow path of theological conservatism, however, other Protestants recognized the need to enlarge the boundaries, especially as the atrocities of the Holocaust, in the course of which the Nazis killed 6 million Jews during World War II, came to light. It was an evil that was, in the words of one Jew, "overwhelming in its scope, shattering in its fury, inexplicable in its demonism." As early as the 1930s, religious leaders began talking about something they called the Judeo-Christian tradition, which was a response to America's growing pluralism. The Temple of Religion at the New York World's Fair in 1938–39 used this notion of the "Judeo-Christian tradition" to exclude other religious groups: Mormons, Buddhists, Jehovah's Witnesses, and a host of others, even pentecostals, whom they regarded as beyond the bounds of American respectability. As the movement evolved in the succeeding decades it asserted a solidarity between Christians and Jews that had been tragically lacking during World War II, and the widespread support for the formation of the state of Israel in 1948 also pointed to a collaboration across the two religious traditions.

The common ground among Jews, Catholics, and Protestants expanded into the realm of popular theology in the post–World War II period. Within the space of just a few years three books appeared—one by a Jewish rabbi, Joshua Liebman, another by a Catholic priest, Fulton J. Sheen, and a third by a Protestant minister, Norman Vincent Peale—all of which offered a kind of feel-good theology for Americans who, in the wake of World War II, were just then settling into their role as world leaders. The most popular of the three, Peale's *The Power of Positive Thinking*, first published in 1952, promised readers that they could "feel better about themselves," and, by extension, Americans could meet the challenges of the postwar world, especially the standoff against Communism, if only they adopted a sunny, "can do" disposition and invoked the help of the "Judeo-Christian" God.

Will Herberg, a theologian at Drew University, gave this Judeo-Christian notion another boost in 1955 with the publication of his book *Protestant, Catholic, Jew.* "American religion and American society would seem to be so closely interrelated as to make it virtually impossible to understand each without reference to the other," Herberg wrote. He enlarged the boundaries of "the American way of life" to include Jews and Roman Catholics, but in so doing he effectively bracketed out all others. "The three great religious communions—Protestantism, Catholicism, and Judaism—constitute the three great American religions," Herberg concluded, "the 'religions of democracy.'"

As Americans confronted what many believed were the perils of pluralism in the 20th century, the notion of a "Judeo-Christian tradition" sounded compelling. It suggested a kind of moral consensus between Christians and Jews that has never really existed, and the use of the term, especially by neoconservatives and by leaders of the Religious Right in the 1980s and 1990s, functioned as a code for exclusion. It implied that Christians and Jews were the "true" Americans and that everyone else—

# The Holocaust Nightmare

*In the years following World War II, Jewish Americans sought to come to terms with the atrocities of the Holocaust. In 1956 Elie Wiesel, a Holocaust survivor who had settled in the United States after the war, published* Night, *a haunting memoir about life in the concentration camps of World War II. This passage describes the first night in camp, an experience that prompted him to call the existence of God into question. Wiesel, who dedicated his life to ensuring that humanity would never forget the horrors of hate and intolerance, was awarded the Nobel Peace Prize in 1986 for being a "messenger to mankind."*

The cherished objects we had brought with us thus far were left behind in the train, and with them, at last, our illusions. Every two yards or so an SS man held his tommy gun trained on us. Hand in hand we followed the crowd. . . .

Never shall I forget that night, the first night in camp, which has turned my life into one long night, seven times cursed and seven times sealed. Never shall I forget that smoke. Never shall I forget the little faces of the children, whose bodies I saw turned into wreaths of smoke beneath a silent blue sky. Never shall I forget those flames which consumed my Faith forever. Never shall I forget that nocturnal silence which deprived me, for all eternity, of the desire to live. Never shall I forget those moments which murdered my God and my soul and turned my dreams to dust. Never shall I forget these things, even if I am condemned to live as long as God Himself. Never.

Hindus, Buddhists, Muslims, Sikhs, Taoists, humanists—professed beliefs outside the mainstream.

At the same time that religious leaders tried to adapt to America's new pluralism by devising the "Judeo-Christian tradition" and expanding the boundaries of acceptable religious life beyond Protestants to Catholics and Jews, Protestant leaders wanted to consolidate in order to avoid duplication of efforts and to present a more united front. This consolidation took the form of the National Council of Churches, an interdenominational organization that was gaveled to order during a snowstorm in Cleveland in November 1949. Even as Protestant leaders had agreed to cooperate, however, they disagreed about the location for the new organization's offices. Powerful forces were pushing for Manhattan, but the magazine *Christian Century,* with offices in Chicago, warned against locating the National Council of Churches in what may have been the only place in America where Protestants came out on the short end of the Protestant-Catholic-Jew formula. The editors argued that the population of New York City included 2.2 million Roman Catholics and 2 million Jews, but fewer than half a million Protestants. "Is the city of New York the appropriate, natural and representative place for the over-all policies and projects of Protestantism to be formulated and administered?" the magazine asked.

If the mainstream was expanding during the middle decades of the 20th century, no religious group took better advantage of the situation than Roman Catholics. American Catholicism went from an "immigrant church" in the 19th century to one that had made a place for itself in America by the latter half of the 20th century. Catholics managed to forge a unified church out of culturally and ethnically diverse elements, so that an Irish parish would not compete with an Italian parish or a German parish or a Hispanic parish. This "Americanization" strategy paid off early in the 20th century as the church became the center of secular activities and socialization for all Catholics; the Catholic Youth Organization, the Knights of Columbus, and a number of social-service agencies were designed to help new immigrants find homes and jobs and adjust to life in America.

The conduct of Roman Catholics during the two World Wars was also crucial. Because many Catholics had come only recently from countries engaged in the European conflicts, the loyalties of these German or Italian Catholics were suspect. Whereas World War I had rekindled some prejudices against Roman Catholics, Catholic men enlisted in the American armed forces in large numbers during World War II, thereby "proving" their patriotism by fighting alongside other Americans. The sons of Roman Catholic immigrants also took full advantage of the GI Bill of Rights, passed by Congress in 1944, which provided discharged soldiers the opportunity to attend college at government expense. With college degrees in hand, the Roman Catholic sons of immigrants then became upwardly mobile in the 1950s and 1960s.

Indeed, Catholic education played a critical role in allowing American Catholics to feel comfortable in American society, and nothing symbolizes their coming of age more than the rise to prominence of the University of Notre Dame, probably the best-known Catholic university in

The National Council of Churches, a coalition of mainline Protestant denominations and the institutional successor to the Federal Council of Churches, was formed in Cleveland during a blizzard in late 1949.

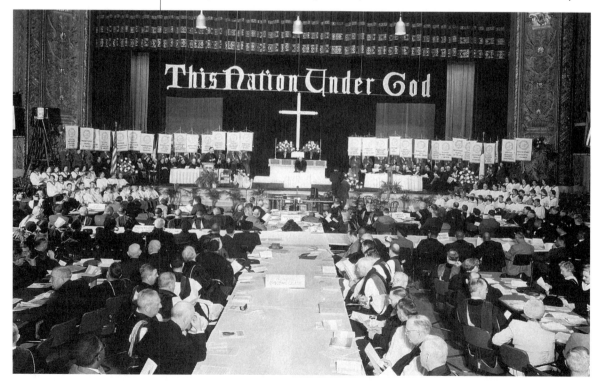

the world. Founded in northern Indiana in 1842 as the Université de Notre Dame du Lac by Edward F. Sorin, a French priest, Notre Dame rose steadily toward academic excellence in the 20th century at the same time that it attracted attention on the athletic field.

Knute Rockne arrived in South Bend, Indiana, as a student and a football player in 1910, helped his team beat Army in 1913, and stayed on at Notre Dame as a chemistry instructor and football coach until his death in 1931. The success of the Fighting Irish on the football field was important because Catholics succeeded in beating the Protestants at their own game; football was first played by students at elite Protestant schools—Princeton, Rutgers, Yale, and Harvard. More important, American Catholics could derive vicarious satisfaction whenever Notre Dame (or Fordham or Holy Cross or Boston College) beat Rutgers or Northwestern or Southern Methodist University on the gridiron—which they did with growing regularity.

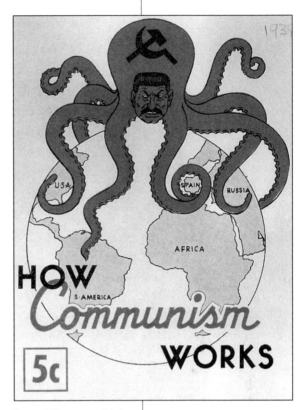

The cover of this 1938 pamphlet published by the Catholic Library Service warns of the tentacular spread of Communism under Joseph Stalin. Opposition to the Soviet Union and its allies determined everything from American foreign policy and military spending to church attendance and public displays of patriotism.

Not all Catholic successes took place on the athletic fields. On the morning of October 4, 1948, a Trappist monk at the Abbey of Our Lady of Gethsemani in Kentucky sent a manuscript off to his literary agent. Father Louis, better known to those in the outside world as Thomas Merton, had been a rowdy undergraduate—and an avowed atheist—at Columbia University before his conversion to Roman Catholicism in 1938. Three years later he became a Trappist, which required that he assume a vow of silence. Merton's manuscript, an autobiography published as *The Seven Storey Mountain,* cast a wary eye on the frenzy of American life, extolled the virtues of contemplation, and criticized the growing secularism of American intellectuals. In the wake of the horrors of the Holocaust and Hiroshima, Merton recommended the solace of the interior and spiritual life.

Members of the University of Notre Dame's football team attend mass at the New York World's Fair in 1965. With success on the gridiron, they regularly beat the Protestants at their own game. Roman Catholics across the United States avidly followed the Fighting Irish.

*The Seven Storey Mountain* became a best-selling book whose commercial success landed its author on the cover of *Time* magazine. Whereas Catholics until the postwar era had been eager to adapt to American culture, Merton's autobiography reflected a growing Catholic maturity, a confidence so great that a Roman Catholic could offer a trenchant critique of American values and the American way of life.

As Roman Catholics began to gain confidence about their place in American society, another religious group, evangelicals, began to enjoy a resurgence at mid-century. The impetus came from an unlikely source—a gangly young preacher just out of Wheaton College, located west of Chicago. William Franklin Graham, reared on a dairy farm near Charlotte, North Carolina, had attended revival meetings conducted by an itinerant evangelist, Mordecai Ham, in 1934 and experienced an evangelical conversion. Billy Graham, who once aspired to be a baseball player, decided instead to attend Bob Jones College (now Bob Jones University) but later transferred to Wheaton, an evangelical liberal-arts college. In 1946 a newly formed organization called Youth for Christ hired Graham, already an accomplished preacher, as its first full-time evangelist.

Graham toured the country (and later the world), preaching to church groups, youth rallies, and stadium gatherings. His charisma and charm, with just a touch of Carolina drawl, opened doors, and his message was beguilingly simple: Repent of your sins, ask Jesus into your heart, and you will be saved. Youth for Christ soon hired another evangelist, Charles B. Templeton, to join Graham on the revival circuit, and they sought to project an air of youthful excitement and enthusiasm. They preferred sport coats to suits and wore loud, colorful ties to emphasize that they were not the stodgy old evangelists of times past. They sought as well to move beyond the separatism and the narrow judgmentalism of the fundamentalists, although their theology remained similar to that of their fundamentalist forebears.

Templeton matched Graham in preaching ability—indeed, many thought that Graham was the lesser preacher of the two men—but Templeton also possessed a restless intellect. He decided to attend Princeton Theological Seminary, and before enrolling he challenged Graham, who also had no formal theological training, to accompany him. Templeton's proposal prompted something of a crisis in young Graham; he pondered the offer at some length but finally decided, while on a spiritual retreat in the San Bernardino Mountains of southern California, to set aside intellectual questions and simply to "preach the gospel."

Although they remained friends for the rest of their lives, the two men followed very different paths. After Templeton graduated from Princeton Seminary in 1951 he became an evangelist for the newly formed National Council of Churches, the federation of mainline—and generally liberal—

Charles Templeton (left) and Billy Graham chat on the platform before the start of a Youth for Christ rally in 1946. The flamboyant young preachers would remain lifelong friends, even after Templeton became an atheist and Graham the best-known preacher of the 20th century.

# An American Monk

*The conversion of Thomas Merton to Roman Catholicism provided American Catholics with an articulate, intelligent, and persuasive spokesman for the faith. In this passage from his autobiography,* The Seven Storey Mountain, *Merton recounts his initial visit to the Trappist Gethsemani monastery, outside Louisville, Kentucky, which he would later join as a monk.*

Thomas Merton, pictured here in 1951, led the life of a rowdy under-graduate at Columbia University before his conversion to Roman Catholicism in 1938.

There were still about three weeks left until Easter. Thinking more and more about the Trappist monastery where I was going to spend Holy Week, I went to the library one day and took down the *Catholic Encyclopedia* to read about the Trappists. I found out that the Trappists were Cistercians, and then, in looking up Cistercians, I also came across the Carthusians, and a great big picture of the hermitages of the Camaldolese.

What I saw on those pages pierced me to the heart like a knife.

What wonderful happiness there was, then, in the world! There were still men on this miserable, noisy, cruel earth, who tasted the marvelous joy of silence and solitude, who dwelt in forgotten mountain cells, in secluded monasteries, where the news and desires and appetites and conflicts of the world no longer reach them.

They were free from the burden of the flesh's tyranny, and their clear vision, clean of the world's smoke and of its bitter sting, was raised to heaven and penetrated into the deeps of heaven's infinite and healing light.

They were poor, they had nothing, and therefore they were free and possessed everything, and everything they touched struck off something of the fire of divinity. And they worked with their hands, silently ploughing and harrowing the earth, and sowing seed in obscurity, and reaping their small harvests to feed themselves and the other poor. They built their own houses and made, with their own hands, their own furniture and their own coarse clothing, and everything around them was simple and primitive and poor, because they were the least and the last of men, they had made themselves outcasts, seeking, outside the walls of the world, Christ poor and rejected of men.

Above all, they had found Christ, and they knew the power and sweetness and the depth and the infinity of His love, living and working in them. In Him, hidden in Him, they had become the "Poor Brothers of God." And for His love, they had thrown away everything, and concealed themselves in the Secret of His Face. Yet because they had nothing, they were the richest men in the world, possessing everything: because in proportion as grace emptied their heart of created desire, the Spirit of God entered in and filled the place that had been made for God. And the Poor Brothers of God, in their cells, they tasted within them the secret glory, the hidden manna, the infinite sweet exultancy of the fear of God, which is the first intimate touch of the reality of God, known and experienced on Earth, the beginning of heaven. The fear of the Lord is the beginning of heaven. And all day long, God spoke to them: the clean voice of God, in His tremendous peacefulness, spending truth within them as simply and directly as water wells up in a spring. And grace was in them, suddenly, always in more and more abundance, they knew not from where, and the coming of this grace to them occupied them altogether, and filled them with love, and with freedom.

And grace, overflowing in all their acts and movements, made everything they did an act of love, glorifying God not by drama, not by gesture, not by outward show, but by the very simplicity and economy of utter perfection, so utter that it escapes notice entirely.

Protestant denominations, but his doubts about the truth of Christianity festered and eventually overwhelmed him. "I came to a point finally where to go on would have meant preaching things I didn't believe," he recalled decades later. In 1957 he returned to his native Toronto and embarked on an illustrious career as a journalist, sports cartoonist, editor, television news director, author, novelist, playwright, and screenwriter.

Graham, on the other hand, having made his momentous decision to "preach the gospel," descended from the San Bernardino Mountains in 1949 and embarked on his Los Angeles crusade. Week after week the crowds flocked to his tent, dubbed the "canvas cathedral," in downtown Los Angeles. He claimed converts from the worlds of politics, music, Hollywood, and even organized crime—individuals who had led sinful, wretched lives but were suddenly made new when they, in Graham's words, "made a decision for Christ." One of Graham's converts, Stuart Hamblen, an actor and singer-songwriter, commemorated his conversion with a song, "It Is No Secret (What God Can Do)," which became popular at revival gatherings.

Aside from the crowds and the conversions in the City of Angels, Graham also caught the eye of newspaper publisher William Randolph Hearst, who was apparently attracted by Graham's strong denunciations of Communism. With a mere two words, "puff Graham," Hearst instructed his newspapers to give the young evangelist lots of favorable publicity. Like a seasoned surfer who caught "the big one," Graham rode the wave of press attention to national prominence, appearing on the cover of *Time* magazine and, in the midst of the cold war, enjoying celebrity status as a clean-cut preacher who defended American middle-class sensibilities against the attacks of what he referred to as "godless Communism."

Graham came to prominence at a unique moment in history, when technological innovations in travel and communications made it possible for him to consider all of the United States (and many parts of the world) as his parish. Whereas the Methodist circuit rider of the previous century traveled by horseback and preached from a soapbox to anyone within earshot, Graham took full advantage of both air transportation and the

airwaves. He hopscotched the country on airplanes and used radio and television to broadcast his sermons to the masses. During his crusade in Portland, Oregon, in 1950, Graham made the decision to form a not-for-profit corporation to handle finances and to organize his crusades. The Billy Graham Evangelistic Association, with its headquarters in Minneapolis, became a well-oiled corporate machine with advance work that would be the envy of any politician. One of Graham's most impressive legacies over a career that extended more than half a century was that no one ever seriously questioned the integrity of his financial dealings or his moral conduct.

As middle-class Americans—Protestants, Catholics, and Jews—basked in postwar prosperity they pushed out of the cities and toward the suburbs. Levittown, New York, a suburban housing development with cookie-cutter architecture and postage-stamp yards, became the prototype for the bedroom communities surrounding the cities. For many Americans in the 1950s belief in God and some kind of religious affiliation were essential ammunition in the cold war that the United States was waging against the Soviet Union and its satellite nations. "America should

A huge tent, dubbed the "canvas cathedral," went up at the corner of Washington and Hill streets in Los Angeles in 1949 for Billy Graham's eight-week-long revival "crusade." His dynamic preaching and boyish good looks attracted thousands of people.

be grateful for the spiritual tide which flows unceasingly into our national life through its institutions of religion," the editors of *Christian Century* exuded in 1951. "This Christian heritage can survive even if our civilization falls." Congress added the words "under God" to the Pledge of Allegiance in 1954, so that thereafter the United States would be "one nation, *under God,* indivisible, with liberty and justice for all."

But America was divided, deeply divided along racial lines, and African Americans did not enjoy "liberty and justice for all." Although northern evangelicals had pressed for the abolition of slavery in the 19th century and had assisted freed blacks after the Civil War, they lost interest after Reconstruction. A cynical system of Jim Crow laws across the South conspired to keep African Americans in a subordinate status, and if blacks stepped out of line there was no shortage of vigilantes to remind them of their place. Lynchings became all too common. More than 1,200 African Americans fell victim to lynch mobs in the final decade of the 19th century, and a thousand more died by lynching between 1900 and 1915, some of them in public spectacles meant to intimidate the entire black community. More than 10,000 people witnessed a lynching in the public square of Waco, Texas, in 1916, for example.

"If it is necessary every Negro in the State will be lynched," James K. Vardaman, governor of Mississippi, declared in one of his more temperate comments about blacks, "it will be done to maintain white supremacy." After Booker T. Washington, an African-American educator and head of the Tuskegee Institute in Alabama, dined with President Theodore Roosevelt at the White House, Ben Tillman, U.S. senator from South Carolina, remarked that it "will necessitate our killing a thousand [Negroes] before they will learn their place again." The Scottsboro case in Alabama, where nine black men were convicted in 1931 of raping two white women on the flimsiest of evidence, underscored that blacks had no guarantee of justice in white-dominated courtrooms.

Although African Americans who migrated to northern cities fared little better, facing poverty, hunger, and the lack of safe, adequate housing, they made steady, albeit slow, progress toward equality in the middle decades of the 20th century. On April 15, 1947, Jackie Robinson became the first black to play major league baseball, and a bit more than a year later President Harry Truman's executive order desegregated the armed forces. On May 17, 1954, the U.S. Supreme Court finally laid the legal groundwork for racial integration with its landmark *Brown* v. *Board of Education of Topeka* ruling.

Reversing the infamous 1896 *Plessy* v. *Ferguson* decision, which had enshrined the notion of "separate but equal" accommodations for blacks and whites, the Court declared that separate facilities for whites and blacks were "inherently unequal," although the Court's implementation order the following year required only a gradual approach to desegregation and left details to local federal judges and school boards. The *Brown* decision nevertheless demonstrated that the strategy of litigation could undermine entrenched southern practices; full desegregation, however, would require the cooperation of blacks to demand the reforms mandated by the Supreme Court.

One African American willing to make demands on behalf of his people was Vernon Johns, pastor of the Dexter Avenue Baptist Church, a middle-class black congregation located near the statehouse in Montgomery, Alabama. Johns found small ways to annoy racists. After police beat a black man, Johns advertised his sermon title for the following Sunday: "It's Safe to Murder Negroes in Montgomery." One day he ordered a sandwich in a white restaurant and, contrary to custom, decided to eat it there rather than take it out, whereupon a gang of customers went to their cars for guns. "I pronounced the shortest blessing of my life over that sandwich," Johns recalled later. "I said, 'Goddam it.'"

Like other African Americans in Montgomery, Johns chafed at the Montgomery bus system, which required blacks to pay their fares to the driver at the front of the bus and then move to the rear or even exit the bus and reboard, behind the "whites only" section. Cynical drivers sometimes drove off after collecting the fare and before the black rider could re-enter at the rear. Johns paid his fare one day and sat in the "whites only" section at the front. The driver refused to move, but Johns demanded—and received—his money back, thereby providing a minor victory for blacks against the Montgomery bus system.

The crippling blow against the segregation of Montgomery buses was delivered, however, by a diminutive woman, Rosa Parks. On December 1, 1955, while Parks was riding home on the Cleveland Avenue line and sitting in the first row of the "colored" section, the driver instructed her to move to the back of the bus to make room for a white patron (a "sliding divider" between whites and blacks would be moved farther back if more whites entered the bus). Parks refused to move and was arrested. The incident fanned the long-smoldering anger of the African-American community, which responded by launching a boycott against the bus system. The local black clergy gathered to form the Montgomery Improvement Association (MIA) to coordinate the boycott, and when it came time to choose a president the meeting turned to the 26-year-old preacher who had succeeded Johns as pastor of the Dexter Avenue Baptist Church. Martin Luther King, Jr., who had been reluctant to get involved in the protest, nevertheless accepted the presidency of the association. "Well, if you think I can render some service," he said, "I will."

King later remarked that the summons to leadership "happened so quickly that I did not have time to think it through. It is probable that if I had I would have declined the nomination." King, the son of a black preacher in Atlanta, had studied at Morehouse College, Crozer Theological Seminary, and Boston University, where he received a Ph.D. in theology in 1955. He had been influenced by the Social Gospel, especially by Walter Rauschenbusch, the Baptist minister who sought social reform in the name of Christianity, and by Mahatma Gandhi's nonviolent strategy for social change. As the Montgomery bus boycott continued into 1956, King attracted notice for his oratorical skills and his courage, although he harbored misgivings, seeking a way to "move out of the picture without appearing a coward."

The boycott was a masterpiece of logistical planning and dogged persistence. For nearly a year the blacks of Montgomery spurned the buses that had so mistreated them and had taken their business for granted.

Some traveled by carpool, but most went on foot, some of them over long distances. The African Americans of Montgomery, in King's words, "came to see that it was ultimately more honorable to walk the streets in dignity than to ride the buses in humiliation."

For King himself the Montgomery boycott shaped the remainder of his career as a theologian, an activist, and a pastor. King was not yet a convinced pacifist when the boycott began. When his house was bombed in late January 1956 he

D. H. Lackey, a deputy sheriff, fingerprints Rosa Parks, a seamstress, after her arrest for refusing to move to the back of a bus in Montgomery, Alabama, on December 1, 1955.

had been seeking a gun permit and had the protection of armed body-guards; a friend described his house as "an arsenal." His views changed, however, as the boycott continued. "Living through the actual experience of the protest, nonviolence became more than a method to which I gave intellectual assent," King said. "It became a commitment to a way of life."

King and other leaders of the MIA were convicted of conspiracy to interfere with the bus company's operations, but in November 1956 they prevailed when the U.S. Supreme Court declared Alabama's segregation laws unconstitutional. Thus emboldened, King and others sought to build on their success. In 1957 they formed the Southern Christian Leadership Conference (SCLC), an organization of black leaders, many of them ministers, who worked for desegregation and civil rights. That same year King, who was chosen president of the new group, articulated the goal of voting rights for blacks during the Prayer Pilgrimage for Freedom at the Lincoln Memorial. King's efforts on behalf of black Americans had now taken him far beyond Montgomery, and by the end of 1959 he resigned from the Dexter Avenue church and moved to Atlanta to devote his full energies to the civil rights movement.

Two white Baptists at a church in Little Rock, Arkansas, turn away black worshipers on October 5, 1958. Some African Americans, emboldened by 1950s court rulings that challenged segregation policies, and responding to Martin Luther King, Jr.'s, observation that 11 o'clock Sunday morning was "the most segregated hour in America," tried to worship in white congregations.

The editors of *Christian Century* had argued that the headquarters for the National Council of Churches be located near what they called the "center of its constituency to insure the maximum response to its leadership," and readers chimed in with suggestions ranging from St. Louis and Chicago to Manhattan, Kansas, and "the southeastern part of Nebraska." Nevertheless, the National Council of Churches chose the Upper West Side of Manhattan for its offices, on a site adjacent to Columbia University overlooking the Hudson River. This neighborhood, known as Morningside Heights, had been a place of refuge for Protestants around the turn of the 20th century. As Jewish and Catholic immigrants overwhelmed the precincts of lower Manhattan late in the 19th century, Protestants steadily constructed their own "city on a hill" in Morningside

Heights, just as the Puritans had sought to carve their city on a hill out of the howling wilderness of Massachusetts in the 17th century.

A steady stream of Protestant institutions moved to the upper West Side: Columbia (originally an Anglican—or Episcopal—school), Union Theological Seminary (Presbyterian), St. Luke's Hospital (Episcopal), Riverside Church (Baptist and Congregational), and the (Episcopal) Cathedral of St. John the Divine, which the architect Ralph Adams Cram intended as a kind of medieval walled city. By the late 1950s the National Council of Churches joined this Protestant pantheon in a hulking, modern building known formally as the Interchurch Center and informally as the "God Box" or the "Protestant Kremlin." All the warnings about isolation from the "psychological center" of American Protestantism went unheeded, and when it came time to lay the cornerstone for the Interchurch Center, which symbolized the fusion of Protestant respectability with the American way of life, the logical choice for the task was President Dwight Eisenhower, who offered a paean to religious liberty and toleration in an age increasingly marked by pluralism.

"In this land, our churches have always been sturdy defenders of the Constitutional and God-given rights of each citizen," Eisenhower declared at the cornerstone-laying ceremony on October 12, 1958. "We are politically free people because each of us is free to express his individual faith." Those maxims would again be tested in the decades ahead as even the Protestant-Catholic-Jew consensus and the Judeo-Christian formula proved inadequate to contain the rising tides of religious pluralism.

*Chapter 4*

# Religion in the New Frontier

Jewish leader Abraham Joshua Heschel (center) marches alongside Martin Luther King, Jr. The civil rights movement stirred the consciences of many Americans, who recognized that black Americans had been denied equal access to the American dream.

Religion played a central role in the 1960 Presidential election. Only once before, in 1928, had a Roman Catholic run for President on a major party ticket, and Alfred E. Smith, the governor of New York, had lost resoundingly to Herbert Hoover. By 1960, however, with Roman Catholics having grown in numbers and having found their place in American society, the prospect of a Catholic President seemed less daunting, especially when the Democratic candidate, John F. Kennedy of Massachusetts, was so bright and charming and articulate—and young. His Republican opponent, Richard M. Nixon, had been Dwight Eisenhower's Vice President. Nixon had forged close ties with the evangelist Billy Graham, who, over the course of a friendship that lasted several decades, probably came as close as anyone to being Nixon's soul-mate.

Although Graham publicly denied any preference in the Presidential election, he took part in a secret meeting of American Protestant leaders in Montreux, Switzerland, in the spring of 1960, when it appeared likely that Kennedy would capture the Democratic nomination. The purpose of the gathering, which included Norman Vincent Peale, pastor of New York City's Marble Collegiate Church, was to discuss ways to deny Kennedy the Presidency and thereby ensure Nixon's election. Although no specific action came from that meeting, the discussion itself drew on deep prejudices.

## What Every American Should Know

### IS CATHOLIC CONTROL POSSIBLE IN AMERICA?

Many people ask "What could a Catholic President do to endanger our right to worship?" The President of the United States could change our entire way of life.

America is bound by the ruling of the Supreme Court on integration or any other matter. The Supreme Court Judges as well as the Federal Judges are appointed by the President. The term of these offices is for life. Let's consider the following facts concerning the highest court in our land:

**Supreme Court Judges may retire at the age of 70, or at the age of 65 after 15 years of service.** All of the vacancies could be filled by Catholics appointed by the President.

| Supreme Court Judges | Age | Took Office |
|---|---|---|
| Hugo Black | 75 * | 1937 |
| William Brennan | 55 | 1956 |
| Harold Burton | 73 * | 1945 |
| Tom Clark | 62 | 1949 |
| William Douglas | 62 * | 1939 * |
| Felix Frankfurter | 79 * | 1939 |
| John Harlan | 62 | 1955 |
| Charles Whittaker | 60 | 1957 |
| Earl Warren | 70 * | 1953 |

*Five of these nine Supreme Court Judges will have reached the retirement age within the next four years. All but two will have reached retirement age in the next eight years.

An organization calling itself Volunteers for the Preservation of Religious Freedom distributed this pamphlet opposing Senator John F. Kennedy's campaign for the Presidency in 1960. Many Protestants warned that a Roman Catholic should not occupy that office because he would be subject to a "foreign power": the pope.

In April 1949 Paul Blanshard, a Congregational minister-turned-atheist, had published *American Freedom and Catholic Power*, which argued that Roman Catholics represented a threat to American democracy because of their loyalty to a "foreign" power, the Vatican. "Unfortunately the Catholic people of the United States are not citizens but *subjects* of their own religious commonwealth," he wrote. "They are compelled by the very nature of their Church's authoritarian structure to accept nonreligious as well as religious policies that have been imposed on them from abroad." Blanshard's call to arms against the supposed threat of Catholicism went through eleven editions in as many months, reminding American Catholics that, despite their advances in American society over the previous decades, many Protestants remained deeply suspicious of their faith.

Kennedy addressed "the religion issue" directly at least three times during the 1960 campaign, responding to Protestant fears that he, as a Catholic, would be obliged to obey the pope on matters of public policy. "I want no votes solely on account of my religion," he declared to a meeting of the Society of American Newspaper Editors, and he reiterated that he was "dedicated to the separation of church and state, to the preservation of religious liberty, to an end to religious bigotry, and to the total independence of the officeholder from any form of ecclesiastical dictation." Later in the campaign, addressing the Ministerial Association in Houston, the Democratic nominee assured Americans that he would not be bullied by any pronouncement from the Vatican. Although some Protestants remained wary of a Roman Catholic in the White House, a majority of Americans—albeit a bare majority in one of the closest elections in U.S. history—voted to break with the past and entrust the nation, in the words of Kennedy's inaugural address, to "a new generation of Americans."

This new generation was more enamored of the future than the past, and Kennedy meant to lead America into that future, which he called the "New Frontier" and which included an enthusiastic embrace of science and technology. Ever since the Scopes trial back in 1925 many Americans had remained wary of science, which, in the wake of Charles Darwin's evolutionary theory, could no longer be counted on to shore up the claims of theology. When the Soviet Union launched *Sputnik,* a tiny satellite, on October 4, 1957, however, Americans' attitudes toward science, especially toward science education, began to change. In 1958 Congress passed the National Defense Education Act, which provided federal money for education in the sciences, and on May 25, 1961, Kennedy set before Congress the goal of a manned landing on the moon "before this decade is out."

Americans responded with a flurry of devotion to science and technology. Kennedy's vision carried Americans forward with a kind of inexorable force, and the future looked bright indeed—a world of interplanetary travel, a world of convenience, a world where science had eradicated hunger and disease. And if Americans needed a demonstration of this Brave New World that awaited them, they looked to a huge shrine in Flushing, New York, the New York World's Fair of 1964–65, with its whirring, futuristic exhibitions that extolled the virtues and the promise of the technological age.

For some Americans the dawn of this new era demanded a new theology, one that broke with the quaint suspicions and prejudices of bygone days. *Time* magazine placed the matter in the starkest terms with a 1966 cover, a black background with large red letters that asked: "Is God Dead?" The "death of God" theology, stated in various ways by a handful of theologians, represented a departure from old religious systems and an embrace of a new self-sufficiency on the part of humanity, which no longer needed the "crutch" of religion. That same year Richard Rubenstein, a rabbi, published *After Auschwitz,* which argued that religion as usual was no longer possible after the Holocaust.

Billy Graham addresses a 1961 Presidential prayer breakfast, attended by John F. Kennedy (right of the American flag) and Vice President Lyndon B. Johnson (at Graham's left). Despite his private opposition during the 1960 campaign to the idea of a Catholic in the White House, Graham embarked on a high-profile friendship with the new President that was politically beneficial to both men.

But the rumors of God's death, to paraphrase Mark Twain, turned out to have been greatly exaggerated. Religious groups responded to the technological age by trying to retool for the new era, and no institution reshaped itself more profoundly in the 1960s than the Roman Catholic Church, an organization not often associated with change. On October 11, 1962, after Pope John XXIII had remarked that the leaders of the church were not meant to be "museum-keepers, but to cultivate a flourishing garden of life," more than 2,000 bishops from around the world gathered at St. Peter's Basilica for a meeting of Roman Catholic leaders known as the Second Vatican Council, or Vatican II. The council lasted more than three years, outlived its convener, John XXIII, and profoundly recast Catholic practice and teachings, from the nature of church authority to the conduct of the mass to the absolving of Jews from any responsibility for the death of Jesus. John XXIII, who was designated *Time* magazine's "Man of the Year" for 1962, resolved that the church should reach out to those he called the "separated brethren," by which he meant non-Catholics, and see them as engaged, knowingly or not, in the process of joining the church, either in this life or the next.

American Catholics saw the changes from Vatican II most clearly in everyday life. Mass was no longer said in Latin, but in the vernacular, the language of the local people, an innovation that soon led to "folk masses," or "guitar masses." Catholics no longer had to observe "meatless Fridays," when they could not consume meat. Nuns were no longer required to dress in habits, and priests forsook the cassock for more conventional trousers.

The Second Vatican Council brought a burst of energy and enthusiasm to the Catholic Church in America, which was now suddenly allowed to experiment with new forms of worship. Consistent with the reforms of Vatican II, the laity assumed a larger role in the affairs of the church, from the formation of parish councils and advisory boards for parochial schools to assisting at the mass. Some interpreted Vatican II as a license to press for further reforms, including the idea of married—or even female—clergy, but conservatives resisted, many using the Latin mass as a rallying point. The Catholic Traditionalist Movement, for example, was founded in 1964, insisting, in defiance of Vatican II, on the use of Latin in Roman Catholic services.

Still other changes racked the Roman Catholic Church in America in the wake of Vatican II. The council expressed a new openness to what the New Testament describes as "Spiritual gifts," ranging from love, joy, and peace to divine healing and even speaking in tongues, a phenomenon associated with pentecostalism. These Spiritual gifts, "whether they be the most outstanding or the more simple and widely diffused," the council declared in its *Dogmatic Constitution on the Church*, "are to be received with thanksgiving and consolation, for they are exceedingly suitable and useful for the needs of the church." In 1967 four members of a lay faculty prayer group at Duquesne University, a Roman Catholic school in Pittsburgh, sought the gifts of the Holy Spirit. Having read *The Cross and the Switchblade,* which detailed the efforts of a pentecostal pastor, David Wilkerson, to convert New York City gang members to Christianity, the Duquesne faculty group attended a pentecostal prayer gathering held in the home of a Presbyterian laywoman. There they received the baptism of the Holy Spirit, including speaking in tongues, reminiscent of the pentecostal revival that took place in Topeka, Kansas, at the beginning of the century.

Although such spiritual enthusiasm is more often associated with churches like the Assemblies of God, the Church of God in Christ, and various independent and storefront congregations, these spiritual expressions had begun to crop up in more established, formal settings. On a Sunday morning in January 1959, for instance, Dennis J. Bennett, an Episcopal priest and rector of St. Mark's Episcopal Church in Van Nuys, California, announced to his stunned parishioners that he had been baptized by the Holy Spirit and had spoken in tongues. The disclosure engendered a reaction in the parish—as Bennett was explaining his Spirit baptism before the congregation, one of his associates removed his vestments and resigned on the spot—a reaction that eventually led to Bennett's resignation. "We're Episcopalians," one relieved parishioner told *Time* magazine, "not a bunch of wild-eyed hillbillies." Bennett accepted an appointment as vicar of St. Luke's, a blue-collar mission in Seattle, which became a kind of beachhead for what became known as the charismatic renewal movement within the Episcopal church.

Similarly, the developments at Duquesne University reverberated throughout the Roman Catholic Church. A February 1967 retreat for faculty and students, which became known as the "Duquesne weekend," affected another thirty or so students, and by early March the movement had spread to the University of Notre Dame, where another weekend of prayer and reflection took place from April 7 to 9. By year's end the Catholic Charismatic Renewal had spread to Michigan State University and to the University of Michigan, and beginning in 1968 Catholic charismatics, those who claimed the gifts of the Holy Spirit, held the first of what became annual meetings at the University of Notre Dame.

By the late 1970s these gatherings, called the National Conference on Charismatic Renewal in the Catholic Church, attracted well in excess of 20,000 participants. At the parish level, the Catholic Charismatic Renewal succeeded in breathing new life into moribund congregations, although its spiritual ardor sometimes proved divisive. The Roman Catholic hierarchy in the United States viewed the renewal movement with some ambivalence. Although the Catholic Charismatic Renewal had revitalized many parishes, the expression of spiritual gifts could also be wildly enthusiastic and, therefore, unpredictable.

No one, however, could have predicted the firestorm of dissent that greeted the papal announcement from Rome on July 29, 1968. Pope Paul VI, John XXIII's successor, issued an official church encyclical, or teaching, on human sexuality called *Humanae Vitae*, "On Human Life." Although Paul VI had been regarded as something of a progressive prior to his elevation to the papacy in 1963, the pace of change unleashed by the Second Vatican Council alarmed him. He sought, for example, to amend some of the Vatican II documents before their publication in order to make the reforms less radical. On the matter of artificial means of birth control the church had long held the position that every act of sexual intimacy between husband and wife must be open to the possibility of procreation; the use of any artificial means of birth control, therefore, violated church teaching. Just as Vatican II had called other doctrines into question, so too the church established a commission to study the possibility of changes to its teachings on birth control.

Although the panel recommended overwhelmingly to allow contraception, Paul VI countermanded the commission and issued *Humanae Vitae*. He hewed to a conservative line and declared that all artificial means of birth control were contrary to church teaching; the pope allowed only the rhythm method, a natural means of birth control, which was quickly derided as "Vatican roulette." The effect of *Humanae Vitae* on

**THE PILL IS A NO-NO**

Pointing his finger in the manner of Uncle Sam's military recruitment pose, an authoritarian Pope Paul VI orders Catholic women not to use the birth-control pill in this 1968 poster.

American Catholicism was devastating. Catholic women, now primarily middle class and upwardly mobile, no longer wanted to be burdened with large families; fewer children, however, also meant fewer priests for the church because many devout families traditionally had designated one of their sons for the priesthood.

Although *Humanae Vitae* may have rested on solid theological ground, it undermined the Vatican's credibility in the eyes of many American Catholics. The pope was widely characterized as being hopelessly out of touch with everyday believers, and for perhaps the first time in history many Catholics could contemplate the possibility of disobeying the pope and still consider themselves good Catholics. For his part, Paul VI was so distressed at the reaction to *Humanae Vitae* that he issued no other encyclicals for the remainder of his papacy.

For the Roman Catholic Church in America, however, the damage had been done. Attendance at weekly mass fell precipitously, from 71 percent of Catholics in 1963 to 50 percent in 1974. Giving declined by almost $2 billion in that time, and parochial school enrollments dipped from 5.6 million in 1965 to 3.5 million a decade later. *Humanae Vitae,* of course, was not entirely to blame. There were other forces at work in the culture—feminism, the sexual revolution, social and political unrest, and a general distrust of authority structures—but there seems to be little reason to dismiss the conclusions of Andrew Greeley, a sociologist and Roman Catholic priest, who declared that, more than anything else, the encyclical accounts for "the disaster of American Catholicism."

Although American Catholics, with their middle-class attainments and with the election of one of their own to the Presidency, had become full-fledged members of American society, African Americans still faced impediments. The 1954 *Brown* v. *Board of Education* decision may have provided the legal groundwork for equality, and the successful Montgomery bus boycott may have demonstrated the effectiveness of cooperation, but equality itself was slow in coming. On Monday, February 1, 1960, four black students from the local agricultural and technical college sat down at the F. W. Woolworth lunch counter in Greensboro, North Carolina. The waiters studiously ignored their requests for service, but the students nevertheless stayed until closing and reappeared the next morning with 25 others. Within two weeks lunch counter sit-ins had spread throughout the South, a direct challenge to Jim Crow laws.

The road to civil rights led from Montgomery to Selma to Birmingham, Alabama, to Albany, Georgia, to Philadelphia, Mississippi, where local Ku Klux Klan members murdered three civil-rights activists, one African American and two Jews, and buried them in an earthen dam. The summons for civil rights had resonated with American Jews, who knew the sting of oppression and racism. Jews had made considerable strides in their quest to become full-fledged citizens, and some Jews had risen to prominence and visibility within American culture. Woodrow Wilson had appointed a Jew, Louis D. Brandeis, to the U.S. Supreme Court in 1916, for example, Hank Greenberg became a star player for the Detroit Tigers, and Americans danced to the big-band music of Benny Goodman.

American Jews, however, still fought against quotas limiting their entry into elite universities, and they struggled against the stigma of prejudice, which occasionally turned violent. On October 12, 1958, the same day that Dwight Eisenhower laid the cornerstone for the Interchurch Center in New York City, a handful of anti-Semites stuck several dozen sticks of dynamite into the wall of Atlanta's Hebrew Benevolent Society, the city's oldest and largest Reform congregation. The blast ripped a huge hole in the building on Peachtree Avenue, sending a message to Jews everywhere and especially to the congregation's rabbi, Jacob Rothschild, who had been a vigorous proponent of civil rights and racial equality.

Although the five suspects in the case, all of them associated with white supremacist groups, were acquitted, the incident only strengthened

Two civil rights activists, one white, one black, sit at a lunch counter in Knoxville, Tennessee, on March 25, 1960, using this nonviolent tactic to struggle against racial inequality. In response to this incident, Tennessee governor Buford Ellington charged that such sitdowns "were instigated and planned by and staged for the convenience of the Columbia Broadcasting System."

A member of the Union of American Hebrew Congregations demonstrates for civil rights by drawing on the biblical command to "love thy neighbor as thyself." From right to left, Rabbi Richard G. Hirsch (director, Religious Action Center of Reform Judaism), Whitney Young (president, National Urban League), and Bishop Stephen Gil Spotswood (African Methodist Episcopal Church) assemble for a march in August 1963.

the resolve of Jewish and other religious leaders. In June 1963, for example, Abraham Joshua Heschel, a Polish-born rabbi who taught at Jewish Theological Seminary, sent a telegram to President Kennedy calling for an effort of "moral grandeur and spiritual audacity" to liberate America from the scourge of racism. Other religious leaders also joined the struggle. Archbishop Iakovos, head of the Greek Orthodox Archdiocese of North and South America, marched alongside Martin Luther King, Jr., demanding civil rights for all Americans.

Despite the cooperation of American Jews and others, the burden of the fight against segregation rested on the shoulders of King, the spiritual and symbolic head of the movement for civil rights. Throughout the struggle King advocated nonviolence, which he had learned from the teachings of Mahatma Gandhi. "The nonviolent approach does not immediately change the heart of the oppressor," King warned. "It first does something to the hearts and souls of those committed to it. It gives them new self-respect; it calls up resources of strength and courage that they did not know they had. Finally, it reaches the opponent and so stirs his conscience that reconciliation becomes a reality."

For blacks in the early 1960s, however, reality was segregation, beatings, the blast of fire hoses, and the assault of snarling police dogs unleashed against civil-rights protestors by Bull Connor, the chief of police in Birmingham, Alabama. A sniper gunned down Medgar Evers, a black civil-rights leader, outside his Jackson, Mississippi, home. "We will turn America upside down in order to turn it right side up," King promised. On August 28, 1963, King and other African-American leaders rallied a quarter of a million blacks (and some whites) for the March on Washington for Jobs and Freedom. The logistics of the demonstration had left King all but exhausted by the time he ascended the dais at the Lincoln Memorial to address the throng. He stumbled woodenly through his prepared remarks, when someone nearby shouted encouragement, "Tell 'em about the dream, Martin!"

In the best tradition of African-American call-and-response preaching, King unleashed an extemporaneous riff. "I have a dream," he cried, and the crowd began cheering. "I have a dream that one day on the red hills of Georgia the sons of former slaves and the sons of former slave owners will be able to sit down together at the table of brotherhood." The audience responded. "I have a dream," he continued, shouting down the thunderous waves of applause, "that even the state of Mississippi, a state sweltering with people's injustices, sweltering with the heat of oppression, will be transformed into an oasis of freedom and justice." The audience was electrified. "I have a dream," he cried again, "that my four little children will one day live in a nation where they will not be judged by the color of their skin but by the content of their character."

The March on Washington stirred the public conscience and prompted the Kennedy Administration to draft legislation in support of civil rights. But real equality for African Americans remained a mirage. At 10:19 on Sunday morning, September 15, 1963, less than a month after King's "I Have a Dream" speech, a bomb ripped through the basement of the Sixteenth Street Baptist Church in Birmingham, killing 4 black children, injuring 20 others, and blowing the face of Jesus out of a stained-glass window. "I cannot sit idly by in Atlanta and not be concerned about what happens in Birmingham," King had written from the solitary-confinement jail cell in Birmingham several months earlier, where he was being held on charges of contempt. "Injustice anywhere is a threat to justice everywhere."

Noting that "we still creep at horse-and-buggy pace toward gaining a cup of coffee at a lunch counter," King, scribbling on the back of scrap paper, replied to his critics, many of them Protestant ministers, who counseled him to avoid confrontation. In so doing, he gave voice to the frustrations of people of color in a white America. "Perhaps it is easy for those who have never felt the stinging darts of segregation to say, 'Wait,'" King wrote, but the time for resistance had finally arrived. African Americans could no longer wait for equality. "There comes a time when the cup of endurance runs over," he concluded, "and men are no longer willing to be plunged into the abyss of despair."

As King mounted his nonviolent crusade for equality, based on his understanding of the Christian faith, other voices in the African-American community drew on other religious traditions. The Nation of Islam built upon such diverse sources as the Moorish Science Temple, the Jehovah's Witnesses, and Marcus Garvey's Universal Negro Improvement Association. Although the precise origins of the Nation of Islam are shrouded in mystery, in the summer of 1930 a light-skinned black man named Wallace D. Fard (also known as Farad Muhammad) circulated in a Detroit ghetto. Fard, who peddled exotic silks and artifacts, told blacks of their "true" heritage as Moors or Arabs and extolled the glorious history of black "Afro-Asia." The Qur'an, not the Bible, was the proper book for the Black Nation, he said, and Christianity had been used by the white man, the "blue-eyed devil," as a tool for the enslavement of blacks.

Fard organized meetings for his followers, and soon they assembled in what he called Temples of Islam. A young black man named Elijah Poole became Fard's most devoted follower and trusted lieutenant, and when Fard disappeared in 1934 Poole, who took the name Elijah Muhammad, assumed leadership of the movement and relocated to the South Side of Chicago. Muhammad declared himself "Prophet" and "Messenger of Allah" and proceeded to build a substantial following in Chicago and other cities. Taking a page from Garvey's teachings on economic self-sufficiency, Muhammad organized various business enterprises around the Chicago temple: a dry-cleaning plant, bakery, clothing stores, grocery stores.

Muhammad spread his teachings through a newspaper, *Muhammad Speaks.* He taught the virtues of hard work, thrift, and the accumulation of wealth. Blacks, he said, must stop looking to whites for jobs and justice, because the white man had conspired to keep the black man sub-servient. The Nation of Islam, however, was prepared to show blacks a better way. The original man, Muhammad taught,

A Black Muslim woman listens intently to an address by Elijah Muhammad, leader of the Nation of Islam, in Chicago in 1974. Many African Americans, especially in the South, joined the civil rights campaign of Martin Luther King, Jr., in the 1950s and 1960s; others responded to Muhammad's separatist teachings.

was black, not white. Light skin, in fact, had been the result of a perverse experiment conducted thousands of years ago, an experiment that had produced a pale-skinned race that was inferior physically, mentally, and morally and therefore unusually susceptible to evil.

Elijah Muhammad's teachings, though not standard Islam, had a powerful effect within the African-American community, especially among black urban males mired in poverty and hopelessness. The ideology of the Nation of Islam helped to explain their predicament, and it sought to replace the "magnolia myth" of black inferiority with the myth of black superiority. No one was affected more profoundly by Muhammad's teachings than a young inmate serving a 10-year sentence for burglary at the Charlestown State Prison in Massachusetts. Malcolm Little was born in Omaha, Nebraska, the son of a Baptist minister and his wife. One of Malcolm's earliest memories was seeing his house burn down as the firefighters stood around and watched; Malcolm's father, who had been a supporter of Marcus Garvey, disappeared under mysterious circumstances two years later. Malcolm went to school in Michigan and,

A policeman armed with a carbine carries a copy of the Nation of Islam newspaper *Muhammad Speaks* near a mosque where eight people had been wounded in an exchange of gunfire with police in August 1965. Some Black Muslims took Malcolm X's statement that they pursue racial justice and equality "by any means necessary" as a call to arms.

after the eighth grade, found his way to Boston, where he "conked" his hair (straightened it, using lye), wore ghetto-style "zoot suits," dated white women, and became involved in drugs, alcohol, gambling, pimping, and burglary.

While in prison he came into contact with the ideas of Elijah Muhammad. "The very enormity of my previous life's guilt prepared me to accept the truth," Malcolm recalled of his prison conversion to the Nation of Islam. "Every instinct of my ghetto jungle streets, every hustling fox and criminal wolf instinct in me, which would have scoffed at and rejected anything else, was struck numb." Malcolm began to read voraciously and undertook to educate himself by copying the entire dictionary. Upon his release from prison in 1952 he became a zealous apostle for the Nation of Islam. Known as Minister Malcolm X, he quickly emerged as the Black Muslims' leading evangelist. "We Muslims believe that the white race, which is guilty of having oppressed and exploited and enslaved our people here in America, should and will be the victims of God's divine wrath," he told an interviewer in 1963; "white people who are also seeing the pendulum of time catching up with them are now trying to join with blacks, or even find traces of black blood in their own veins, hoping that it will save them from the catastrophe they see ahead. But no devil can fool God."

"The world since Adam has been white—and corrupt," he continued. "The world of tomorrow will be black—and righteous. In the white world there has been nothing but slavery, suffering, death and colonialism. In the black world of tomorrow, there will be *true* freedom, justice and equality for all." Malcolm reserved special contempt for those he called the "Negro preachers," the black Christian ministers who, he believed, had conspired in brainwashing the black man. Such rhetoric, of course, placed him at odds with Martin Luther King, Jr., and his nonviolent movement for racial integration. For Malcolm, following the teachings of Elijah Muhammad, desegregation was just another ploy on the part of whites, in partnership with the "Negro preachers," to keep blacks in servitude. "Christ wasn't white," Malcolm declared. "Christ was black. The poor, brainwashed Negro has been made to believe Christ was white to maneuver him into worshiping white men."

As Malcolm's influence grew in black America, he heard murmurings of sexual and financial improprieties on the part of his mentor, whom he unfailingly referred to as "the Honorable Elijah Muhammad." At first, Malcolm refused to believe the rumors, but as the evidence mounted he also detected that Muhammad was turning against him. In March 1964 Malcolm X broke with the Nation of Islam, and shortly thereafter he took a *hajj* (pilgrimage) to the Muslim holy city of Mecca, where he was exposed to representatives of worldwide Islam and was impressed by their lack of racial bias. By the time Malcolm returned to the United States he had renounced the black supremacist teachings of the Nation of Islam and had taken a new name, El-Hajj Malik el-Shabazz, which commemorated his pilgrimage and his conversion to mainstream Islam. He feared for his life, however, especially after his home on Long Island was firebombed, and on February 21, 1965, as he began a speech at the Audubon Ballroom in upper Manhattan, three gunmen in the front row stood and riddled him with 16 bullets.

More than 22,000 people came to view the body of Malcolm X, the man who had given a voice and a theology to so many African Americans in the 1960s. Malcolm had inspired ideologies as diverse as black economic advancement and the radical Black Panther movement, which sought the overthrow of American social and political institutions. In 1969, for example, James Forman, on behalf of the National Black Economic Development Conference, a group of African Americans seeking

# A Black Man's Conversion

*Born Malcolm Little in Omaha, Nebraska, Malcolm X lived the life of a street hustler before his arrest and conviction on burglary charges. While imprisoned in Massachusetts, he encountered the teachings of Elijah Muhammad, leader of the Nation of Islam. This passage, from the acclaimed* Autobiography of Malcolm X, *recounts his powerful conversion to the Nation of Islam.*

"The true knowledge," reconstructed much more briefly than I received it, was that history had been "whitened" in the white man's history books, and that the black man had been "brainwashed for hundreds of years." Original Man was black, in the continent called Africa where the human race had emerged on the planet Earth.

The black man, original man, built great empires and civilizations and cultures while the white man was still living on all fours in caves. "The devil white man," down through history, out of his devilish nature, had pillaged, murdered, raped, and exploited every race of man not white.

Human history's greatest crime was the traffic in black flesh when the devil white man went into Africa and murdered and kidnapped to bring to the West in chains, in slave ships, millions of black men, women, and children, who were worked and beaten and tortured as slaves.

The devil white man cut these black people off from all knowledge of their own kind, and cut them off from any knowledge of their own language, religion, and past culture, until the black man in America was the earth's only race of people who had absolutely no knowledge of his true identity.

In one generation, the black slave women in America had been raped by the slavemaster white man until there had begun to emerge a homemade, handmade, brainwashed race that was no longer even of its true color, that no longer even knew its true family names. The slavemaster forced his family name upon this raped-mixed race, which slavemaster began to call "the Negro."

This "Negro" was taught of his native Africa that it was peopled by heathen, black savages, swinging like monkeys from trees. This "Negro" accepted this along with every other teaching of the slavemaster that was designed to make him accept and obey and worship the white man.

And where the religion of every other people on Earth taught its believers of a God with whom they could identify, a God who at least looked like one of their own kind, the slavemaster injected his Christian religion into this "Negro." This "Negro" was taught to worship an alien God having the same blond hair, pale skin, and blue eyes as the slavemaster.

This religion taught the "Negro" that black was a curse. It taught him to hate everything black, including himself. It taught him that everything white was good, to be admired, respected, and loved. It brainwashed this "Negro" to think he was superior if his complexion showed more of the white pollution of the slavemaster. This white man's Christian religion further deceived and brainwashed this "Negro" to always turn the other cheek, and grin, and scrape, and bow, and be humble, and to sing, and to pray, and to take whatever was dished out by the devilish white man; and to look for his pie in the sky, and for his heaven in the hereafter while right here on Earth the slavemaster white man enjoyed *his* heaven.

*Malcolm X addresses a Nation of Islam rally in Harlem in 1963. Following his parole in 1952 he quickly became the group's leading evangelist.*

Many a time, I have looked back, trying to assess, just for myself, my first reactions to all this. Every instinct of the ghetto jungle streets, every hustling fox and criminal wolf instinct in me, which would have scoffed at and rejected anything else, was struck numb. It was as though all of that life merely was back there, without any remaining effect, or influence. I remember how, some time later, reading the Bible in the Norfolk Prison Colony library, I came upon, then I read, over and over, how Paul on the road to Damascus, upon hearing the voice of Christ, was so smitten that he was knocked off his horse, in a daze. I do not now, and I did not then, liken myself to Paul. But I do understand his experience.

economic justice, occupied the offices of the National Council of Churches in New York and issued a Black Manifesto "To the White Christian Churches and the Synagogues in the United States and to All Other Racist Institutions." The manifesto demanded $500 million in reparations "to the black people of this country." "Brothers and sisters, we are no longer shuffling our feet and scratching our heads," the manifesto read, echoing the sentiments of both Malcolm X and Martin Luther King, Jr., "We are tall, black and proud."

The decade of the 1960s, which had opened with such promise, ended with widespread disillusion. John Kennedy's soaring rhetoric about the torch being passed to a new generation gave way to riots in the ghettos of Newark, Detroit, and Los Angeles and protests against a war in Vietnam that sapped the resources of the nation and sent more than 58,000 young Americans to their death. The promises of scientific and technological advances were being squandered on weapons of destruction, as the United States and the Soviet Union continued to regard each other with wary eyes. The young President was slain on November 22, 1963, and less than five years later his brother Robert, who was regarded by many as a source of hope for those less privileged, also fell to an assassin's bullet.

The death of Malcolm X deprived the African-American community of a powerful spokesman who had provided a compelling religious vision, and when shots rang outside a motel room in Memphis, Tennessee, on April 4, 1968, one of the nation's most forceful advocates for religious conscience lay in a pool of blood. In his final sermon, delivered the previous day, Martin Luther King, Jr., had sounded a note of hope that "something is happening in our world." He speculated about a conversation he might have with God about which age in history King would choose to inhabit. "Strangely enough, I would turn to the Almighty and say, 'If you allow me to live just a few years in the second half of the twentieth century, I would be happy,'" King responded to his own hypothetical question. "Now that's a strange statement to make, because the world is all messed up. The nation is sick. Trouble is in the land. Confusion all around. That's a strange statement. But I know, somehow, that only when it is dark enough, can you see the stars."

"We need all of you," King continued, especially ministers of the gospel. "Who is it that is supposed to articulate the longings and aspirations of the people more than the preacher? Somehow the preacher must be an Amos, and say, 'Let justice roll down like waters and righteousness like a mighty stream.'" In the days and weeks that followed many people wondered if King had a premonition of his own death. "We've got some difficult days ahead. But that doesn't matter with me now. Because I've been to the mountaintop," he concluded. "I just want to do God's will. And He's allowed me to go up to the mountain. And I've looked over. And I've seen the promised land. I may not get there with you. But I want you to know tonight, that we, as a people, will get to the promised land."

Thousands of buildings were looted or burned in the 1967 Detroit riot. It took National Guardsmen and police almost a week to quell the violence, in which hundreds of people were injured and 43 lost their lives.

*Chapter 5*

# Religion in an Age of Upheaval

Many Americans in the 1960s conducted a kind of courtship with science and technology, a romance that reached its symbolic zenith in the exhibitions of the New York World's Fair of 1964–65 and in Neil Armstrong's step onto the moon on July 20, 1969. But while science offered glimpses of a brave new world of technological advances, other Americans began to harbor second thoughts, and they used the language of religion and theology to express their discontent. By the mid-sixties the younger generation was becoming disillusioned with the war in Vietnam, with the burgeoning "military-industrial complex" of weapons production, with technology itself, and with their parents' religion, which they saw as tied into everything that was wrong with American society: too big, too impersonal, too authoritative, too unresponsive.

A period of unrest shook America to its very foundations as the younger generation took to the streets to demonstrate their impatience with the "establishment." Trust no one over thirty, they declared. Some burned their draft cards, some burned their bras, some burned their college campuses—all of which were seen as symbols of oppression. On August 15, 1969, more than 300,000 rock 'n' roll fans descended on Max Yasgur's farm fields near Bethel, New York, for the Woodstock Music Festival, billed as "Three Days of Peace and Music." Bob Dylan's refrain "the

John Lennon looks up to the white-robed Maharishi Mahesh Yogi in a hotel suite with (from left) Paul McCartney, Ringo Starr, and George Harrison with their wives or girlfriends. The fame of his disciples the Beatles brought the Maharishi international prominence.

times they are a-changin'" turned out to be not only the anthem of an entire generation but the understatement of the decade.

The war in Southeast Asia remained the flashpoint for dissent and bitterness. Philip and Daniel Berrigan, Roman Catholic priests and antiwar activists, broke into Defense Department offices, where they poured blood over files and sabotaged military hardware. Despite Richard Nixon's 1968 campaign promise that he had a plan to end the war in Vietnam, the battle continued, not only in Southeast Asia but also on the campuses and in the coffee shops of America. Dueling bumper stickers declared "AMERICA: LOVE IT OR LEAVE IT" and "AMERICA: CHANGE IT OR LOSE IT." Students erupted in protest across the country, from Berkeley, California, to New York City and also in Madison, Wisconsin, and Iowa City, Iowa. On May 4, 1970, twenty-eight Ohio National Guardsmen fired into a group of antiwar protesters at Kent State University in Ohio, leaving four students dead, permanently paralyzing another, and wounding eight others, thus reminding the nation yet again of its profound divisions.

"There is a revolution coming," Charles Reich, a social critic, warned in *The Greening of America,* published the same year. "It is now spreading with amazing rapidity, and already our laws, institutions and social structure are changing in consequence. It promises a higher reason, a more human community and a new and liberated individual. Its ultimate creation will be a new and enduring wholeness and beauty—a renewed relationship of man to himself, to other men, to society, to nature and to the land." Although the immediate reality looked rather different, many Americans, especially the younger generation, turned to the East for religious inspiration, in part out of disillusionment with Western religions and in part for the novelty of Hinduism, Sikhism, Buddhism, Zen Buddhism, Taoism, Hare Krishna, or even Transcendental Meditation.

"The various wisdoms of the West, religious, philosophical, and scientific, do not offer much guidance to the art of living," Alan Watts, a philosopher and popularizer of Zen Buddhism, explained, "and we find the prospects of making our way in so trackless an ocean of relativity rather frightening." The spirituality of the East, Watts declared, "has the special merit of a mode of expressing itself which is as intelligible—or perhaps as baffling—to the intellectual as to the illiterate, offering possibilities of communication which we have not explored."

Perhaps so, but American culture has a way of leaving its unique stamp on every religious tradition, homegrown or exotic, it adopts. In North America, Buddhist practice, traditionally associated with the monastic life, emphasized meditation more than monasticism, making it more accessible to the middle classes, who were unlikely to exchange their suburban lives for the rigors of a Tibetan monastery. Hare Krishna devotees, who shaved their heads (except for a ponytail), wore saffron-colored robes, and espoused a variation of Hinduism, patrolled airports and street corners seeking converts. Transcendental Meditation (TM), a discipline of meditation developed by Maharishi Mahesh Yogi, who claimed the Beatles among his followers, offered lectures on American campuses. The saffron-robed evangelists and the clean-cut TM lecturers became the most visible practitioners of South Asian religions in America, despite the fact that they represented small minorities back in India.

Many Americans, in their time-honored tradition of openness to new religious ideas, simply absorbed these new religious forms alongside their more traditional involvement with Judaism or Christianity. Others, especially those identified with the counterculture, saw Eastern religions as a fitting complement to the dictum of Harvard professor–turned–drug advocate Timothy Leary: "Tune in, turn on, drop out."

By the early 1970s, however, the drug culture had taken its toll. "The center was not holding," Joan Didion, a perceptive social observer, warned in a haunting essay about the counterculture and life at the end of the 1960s. "Adolescents drifted from city to torn city, sloughing off both the past and the future as snakes shed their skins, children who were never

Alan Watts, a former Episcopal priest, advocated Eastern mysticism as an alternative to Western religions. Here, he shows his affinity for Asian ways in wearing a kimono, removing his shoes, and kneeling on a meditation cushion.

taught and would never now learn the games that had held the society together. People were missing. Parents were missing. Those left behind filed desultory missing-persons reports, then moved on themselves."

About this time a preacher named Chuck Smith accepted an invitation to become pastor of Calvary Chapel, a small congregation of 25 contentious people in Costa Mesa, California. Smith's approach to Christianity was simply to open the Bible and begin teaching. People responded, and the congregation, which had been on the verge of disbanding, began to expand at the rate of 5 percent a week. The largest increase came from an unlikely source: the hippies roaming the beaches of southern California. "My wife and I used to go over to Huntington Beach and park downtown to watch the kids and pray for them," Smith recalled many years later. "We wanted somehow to reach them, but we didn't know how."

Smith confessed that "these long-haired, bearded, dirty kids going around the streets repulsed me," but he decided to try to lure them to his Bible studies. It worked. "At the time I learned about Calvary Chapel I was living down in Laguna Beach where there was a different representative of every faith on just about every corner," recalled Oden Fong, an early convert. "You could walk down the street and talk to a Zen Buddhist, walk a bit farther and see a Krishna, a little farther and see a Satanist." Fong and many others found, in his words, "compassion and love" at Calvary Chapel, and the word spread to other disenchanted hippies in southern California.

Some claimed instantaneous healing, both spiritual and physical, including release from drug and alcohol dependencies, when they converted to evangelical Christianity. Smith welcomed them, all of them, into his congregation, and, unlike many other churches, he accepted them with their long hair, beards, and Levi's. At about the same time that Judy Collins's recording of "Amazing Grace" rocketed to the top of the music charts, the "Jesus People" phenomenon began to attract notice, especially Calvary Chapel's large gatherings on the beach at Corona del Mar, near Newport Beach. Hundreds of reformed hippies, eager to recast their lives, participated in the ancient Christian rite of baptism, so rich in symbolism. Smith and what became known as the Jesus movement provided a

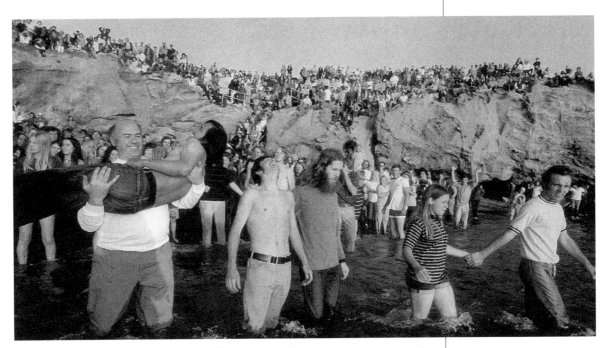

Calvary Chapel pastor Chuck Smith carries a young paralytic into the Pacific during a mass baptism at Corona del Mar, California, in 1971.

kind of halfway house for these disillusioned radicals, easing them gently back onto the road of middle-class respectability.

As many hippies embraced various forms of Eastern religion and others gravitated back to Christianity in the early 1970s, the traditions they encountered were themselves being reshaped by the upheaval of the previous decade. African-American theologians, emboldened by the teachings of Malcolm X and Martin Luther King, Jr., challenged the racism of most religious institutions, invoking King's observation that eleven o'clock Sunday morning was the most segregated hour in America. On February 27, 1973, about 200 armed Native Americans occupied Wounded Knee, South Dakota, the site of a massacre of the Sioux by federal troops in 1890. The occupation, which lasted 71 days and led to 2 deaths and more than 300 arrests, nevertheless served to galvanize Native Americans. Many of them came to recognize that the "white man's religion" had deprived them of their own rich cultural and religious heritage and that the way to recover their cultural identity lay in reclaiming their religious practices, including such rituals as the Sun Dance and the sweat-lodge ceremonies.

If our people
fight
one tribe
at a time,
all will be
killed.
They can
cut off our
fingers
one by one,
but if
we join together
we will
make
a powerful fist.

--Sitting Bull

This 1970 poster calls forth the 19th-century wisdom of Sioux warrior Sitting Bull, using his words and photograph to urge Indian unity against white oppressors. In the wake of black Americans' struggle for civil rights, other Americans began to demand theirs.

An even larger revolution emanated from the women's movement and the sexual revolution. The 1963 publication of Betty Friedan's *The Feminine Mystique,* an attack on male domination in American society, touched off the feminist movement, as women began to challenge the strict—and confining—gender roles that had emerged after World War II. "There was a strange discrepancy between the reality of our lives as women and the image to which we were trying to conform," Friedan wrote. "These problems cannot be solved by medicine, or even by psychotherapy," Friedan concluded, adding that women needed to break free of the ties of the household and enter the academy and the workplace. "We need a drastic reshaping of the cultural image of femininity that will permit women to reach maturity, identity, completeness of self, without conflict with sexual fulfillment."

For many Americans, however, sexual fulfillment and sexual expression were fraught with danger, and despite the affinities between the women's movement and the sexual revolution, the two sometimes collided, especially over the issue of women's bodies. In December 1953, when Hugh Hefner founded *Playboy* magazine, which featured photographs of scantily clad women, he heard protests not only from religious leaders but from women, who accused him of exploitation. The sexual revolution itself may be traced to June 16, 1964, at a club called the Condor in the North Beach neighborhood of San Francisco. As the Republican National Convention was convening across town, Carol Doda, a dancer at the Condor, removed her brassiere and, in becoming a topless dancer, touched off the sexual revolution. The widespread availability—and increased reliability—of birth control and the hippies' defiance of the older generation's definition of morality gave rise to the "free love" and the sexual exhibitionism of the counterculture.

By the 1970s the old rules dictating gender roles and governing sexual behavior no longer applied for many Americans, even for those who considered themselves religious. Catholic women widely disregarded the pope's teaching against the use of artificial birth control, and the old taboos about sexual relations outside of marriage, especially premarital sex, were called into question. Rosemary Radford Ruether, a feminist theologian, identified sin with the "depersonalizing of women." The challenge facing women was to assert their independence from men and from religious institutions that had made them second-class citizens. "Salvation cannot appear save as the resurrection of woman," she wrote in 1973, "that is, in woman's self-definition as an autonomous person."

As women began their long struggle for acceptance and equality in education and commerce, some also began agitating for women to be ordained into the clergy. Since at least the late 17th century women have outnumbered men in the churches, often shouldering the burden of church work, especially religious education. Although Antoinette Brown had been ordained by the small Congregational church in South Butler, New York, in 1853, and pentecostals ordained women as missionaries and pastors early in the 20th century, women had generally been denied access to the ordained ministry.

In 1956 the northern Presbyterians approved the ordination of women to the ministry, and in the 1960s, falling before the juggernaut of the women's movement, the barriers to women's ordination tumbled in rapid succession. The formation of the United Methodist Church in 1968 (from the merger of the Methodist Episcopal Church and the Evangelical and United Brethren Church) guaranteed women access to ordination, and most Lutherans agreed to do the same in 1970. On June 2, 1972, Hebrew Union College, the seminary of the Reform branch of Judaism, generally considered the most liberal, ordained Sally Priesand the first female rabbi in the United States.

Members of the Episcopal Church of the Advocate in Philadelphia take part in communion following the ordination, against church regulation, of eleven women on July 29, 1974. The local event forced a vote on the issue at the general convention, which ruled in favor of women's ordination two years later.

"For thousands of years women in Judaism had been second-class citizens," Priesand recalled later, "they were not permitted to participate fully in the life of the synagogue." As she sat in the historic Plum Street Temple in Cincinnati awaiting her ordination, Priesand took satisfaction in the knowledge that "one more barrier was about to be broken." Sandy Eisenberg became the first female rabbi in Reconstructionist Judaism two years later. In Philadelphia on July 29, 1974, three bishops of the Episcopal church, in a break with their denomination's teachings and tradition, ordained eleven women deacons to the priesthood, much to the dismay of conservatives within the denomination. In September 1976 the General Convention of the Episcopal Church approved the ordination of women to the priesthood, although conservatives continued their opposition for decades thereafter.

The women's movement even affected Mormons and Roman Catholics, two religious groups not known for feminist sympathies. The hierarchy of the Roman Catholic Church maintained its opposition to women's ordination, but the shortage of priests and nuns meant that the church relied more and more heavily on women for the operation of its schools, its social-service agencies, and even its worship services, especially in rural areas. Among Mormons, Sonia Johnson, who billed herself as a housewife and mother, openly supported the proposed equal rights amendment (ERA) to the U. S. Constitution, a position that placed her at odds with the teachings of the Church of Jesus Christ of Latter-day Saints. Johnson's defiance of Mormon officials brought her a measure of notoriety and emboldened her to declare a largely symbolic candidacy for President. The church tried and excommunicated her for heresy in 1979; her Presidential campaign, of course, was unsuccessful.

Someone else had his eyes on the Presidency, a little-known one-term governor of Georgia who billed himself as a peanut farmer. When Jimmy Carter declared his candidacy for the Democratic nomination, few took him seriously. The Presidential campaign of 1976 promised to be eventful, and it represented a ripe opportunity for the Democrats, who had lost the previous election by a landslide. The United States, still reeling from the chaos of the counterculture and struggling to extricate itself from the war in Southeast Asia, had endured the ordeal of the Watergate scandal and the resignation of Richard Nixon. Cynicism was rampant, and nothing made sense—as when the Nobel Committee awarded its 1973 Peace Prize to Henry Kissinger, who as Nixon's secretary of state was the man most responsible for widening the hostilities in Southeast Asia. Gerald Ford, a former congressman from Michigan who had ascended to the Presidency on August 9, 1974, pardoned Nixon in the interest of putting the Watergate nightmare to rest, but that action provoked outrage and piqued public interest in a candidate who was not a Washington insider.

Carter fit that description. He campaigned tirelessly in the precincts of Iowa and the small towns of New Hampshire with his message that he would restore to the nation "a government as good as its people."

At Hill Cumorah in New York, advocates for the equal rights amendment to the Constitution demonstrate against the Mormon church's opposition to their cause. Sonia Johnson, a Mormon housewife, created a stir within the Church of Jesus Christ of Latter-day Saints by supporting the amendment.

Throughout the campaign Carter unabashedly declared that he was a "born-again Christian" and that he taught Sunday school at his Southern Baptist church back in Plains, Georgia. Although he faced a formidable field in the Democratic primaries and a spirited campaign from Ford, Carter's oft-repeated promise that he would "never knowingly lie to the American people" proved irresistible to an electorate wearied of Nixon's relentless prevarications.

The media were entranced by what they believed was the novelty of an evangelical Christian running for President, and they jumped on his statement in a *Playboy* interview that he had "looked on a number of women with lust" and had "committed adultery in my heart many times." That statement was rather unremarkable among evangelicals, who draw a careful distinction between temptation and sin, but the media treated it as newsworthy. In large measure because of Carter's self-description as an evangelical Christian, *Newsweek* magazine declared 1976 "the year of the evangelical," drawing attention to a movement that encompassed somewhere between 25 and 46 percent of the United States population, depending on the poll (the Gallup organization pegged the number at 50 million in 1976). The significance of the Carter campaign was not that an avowed evangelical was running for President; William Jennings Bryan had captured the Democratic nomination three times, to cite only one precedent. The significance lay in the fact that, for the first time in several decades, evangelicals—especially Southern evangelicals—were participating in the political process.

The Scopes trial of 1925 had convinced American evangelicals that the larger world was corrupt and hostile to their interests, and they had responded by retreating from that world into a subculture of churches, denominations, Bible institutes, and colleges of their own making. They regarded politics as tainted, an arena unworthy of the true believer. In 1965, for example, Jerry Falwell, who would become one of the most prominent leaders of the Religious Right, declared that he "would find it impossible to stop preaching the pure saving gospel of Jesus Christ, and begin doing anything else—including fighting Communism, or participating in civil-rights reforms."

Carter's campaign for the Presidency, half a century after the Scopes trial, began to change that. He lured evangelicals, many of whom were Southern Baptists like himself, into the political arena. He spoke their language and represented their values. Ironically, however, despite Carter's unequivocal stand for human rights and his brokering of the historic Camp David peace agreement between Israel and Egypt in 1978, many of the same evangelicals who had supported him in 1976 began to turn against him. Politically conservative evangelicals, emboldened by their influence at the polls, began to make more demands, but a little-known incident turned them against Carter. When his administration's Justice Department sought to enforce antidiscrimination laws at Bob Jones University, a fundamentalist school in Greenville, South Carolina, many evangelicals regarded this as governmental incursion into the evangelical subculture, which had been so carefully constructed in the decades following the Scopes trial. They became bitterly antagonistic toward the President.

Carter was, in a way, then, responsible for the rise of the Religious Right. Once politically conservative evangelicals had mobilized against

In Potlatch, Washington, west of Olympia, Christians turned an abandoned gas station into their meeting hall during the Arab oil embargo in the winter of 1973–74. Many gas stations closed, and Americans endured long lines at others. The event fueled anti-Arab sentiment in the United States.

what they regarded as federal interference at Bob Jones University, they cast about for other issues. According to Paul Weyrich, one of the architects of the Religious Right, the political agenda began to take shape during a conference call among evangelical political leaders in the late 1970s. After discussing their success in forming a coalition in the Bob Jones case, someone asked for suggestions about other matters. Someone else said, "How about abortion?"

Throughout the 1980s and 1990s the leaders of the Religious Right were fond of saying that the Supreme Court's 1973 decision to legalize abortion was the catalyst for their political activity. They also liked to cast themselves as the 20th-century counterparts to the abolitionist crusaders of the 19th century. The reality, however, was more complicated. When the Supreme Court handed down the *Roe* v. *Wade* decision, which removed most legal barriers to abortion, on January 22, 1973, the bishops of the Roman Catholic Church protested, but evangelicals offered nary a whimper. The Southern Baptist Convention, in fact, endorsed the Court's ruling because it saw abortion as a moral rather than a legal or a political matter; the Southern Baptists also applauded the *Roe* decision because it upheld the separation of church and state, a hallmark of Baptist convictions dating back to Roger Williams in the 17th century.

For the leaders of the Religious Right, busily cobbling together a political agenda, however, opposition to abortion fit perfectly. It allowed them to protest what they saw as a society that, dating back to the 1960s, had been far too permissive. Despite the fact that evangelicals had been at the forefront of social-reform movements and campaigns for women's suffrage in the 19th century, evangelicals had resisted the feminist movement in the 1960s. They were uncomfortable with the "free love" of the counterculture, and rising divorce rates in the 1970s persuaded them that the family was imperiled. For the overwhelmingly male leadership of politically conservative evangelicals, moreover, abortion symbolized everything that was wrong with America: women entering the workplace in large numbers, expressing themselves sexually outside of marriage, and then refusing to deal with the consequences, choosing abortion rather than responsibility.

# The Origins of the Religious Right

*Paul Weyrich, head of the Free Congress Foundation, a conservative lobbying organization, was one of the architects of the Religious Right. He recognized that politically conservative evangelicals represented a powerful voting bloc, and he sought to include them in a conservative political coalition. These remarks, presented at a conference in Washington, D.C., in 1991, shed light on the origins of the movement that became known as the Religious Right.*

Most people who comment on the evangelical movement picture it as an offensive movement politically. It is not. It is a defensive movement. The people who are involved in it didn't want to get involved; they got involved very reluctantly. They had accepted the notion (which may have taken root historically at the Scopes trial) that a good Christian would raise his family in the proper manner and would not participate very much in public life. If you did that, you could avoid all the corruption that was manifest in politics. . . .

What caused the movement to surface was the federal government's moves against Christian schools. This absolutely shattered the Christian community's notion that Christians could isolate themselves inside their own institutions and teach what they pleased. The realization that they could not then linked them up with the long-held conservative view that government is too powerful and intrusive, and this linkage was what made evangelicals active. It wasn't the abortion issue; that wasn't sufficient. It was the recognition that isolation simply would no longer work in this society.

As America headed into the 1980 elections the Religious Right, which included such organizations as Moral Majority and the Traditional Values Coalition, brought to the table a compelling message, one calculated to appeal to many Americans already fearful because of the economic woes of high oil prices and skyrocketing interest rates. Following the Iranian seizure of the United States embassy in Teheran in 1979, the evening news carried daily footage of Americans held hostage, taunted by their captors. In this climate of fear many evangelicals were prepared finally to shed their political indifference. "When I started Moral Majority, I was leading the evangelical church out from behind their walls," Jerry Falwell recounted in 1996. His 1980 book, *Listen America!,* warned that there was "no doubt that the sin of America is severe" and that the United States was "literally approaching the brink of national disaster." America must return to Jesus, the leaders of the Religious Right declared, many of them on their own television programs. They decried what they called moral decay in America—divorce, promiscuity, abortion, the Supreme Court decisions in the early 1960s outlawing prayer in public schools—and promised that "God will bless America when America blesses God."

For several weeks late in the summer of 1978 the eyes of the world shifted to the Vatican. Pope Paul VI, who had headed the Roman Catholic Church during the post–Vatican II years and who had issued the disastrous *Humanae Vitae* encyclical in 1968, died at Castel Gandolfo, the papal retreat, on August 6, 1978. The College of Cardinals assembled from around the world to select a successor, and eventually they chose Albino Luciani, the patriarch of Venice, who took the name John Paul I, in honor of his two immediate predecessors, Paul VI and John XXIII. The cardinals had barely returned home when word came that John Paul I himself had died only 33 days into his papacy.

Once again the cardinals assembled and, having just chosen an Italian, they felt free to search more broadly. They turned to a surprise candidate, the reluctant Karol Wojtyla, archbishop of Kraców, who became the first non-Italian pope since Hadrian VI had been elected in 1523. After considering the name Stanislaus, after the patron saint of Kraców, Wojtyla followed his predecessor's example and chose John Paul II. "To the See of

Peter there succeeds today a bishop who is not Roman, a bishop who is a son of Poland," the pope declared at his investiture. "Pray for me! Help me to be able to serve you!"

The new pontiff, the first Slav ever elected to the papacy, was a remarkable man. He spoke a dozen or more languages and brought an unprecedented energy to the papacy. Having been reared under the Communist regime in Poland, he understood firsthand the corruptions and the oppressions of Marxist-inspired government, which claimed to defend the people but which had degenerated into totalitarianism. John Paul II took a dim view of the "liberation theology" so popular among Roman Catholic priests in Latin America because that ideology relied on Marxism. In 1979 he made a return visit to his native Poland, then still under Communist control, and prayed that the Holy Spirit might renew the face of "this earth," meaning Poland. As the Soviet empire teetered and then fell a decade later, John Paul could take satisfaction that his prayer had been answered.

More than any pope in history, John Paul II understood the value of public relations. Though conservative on matters of doctrine—he opposed abortion and artificial means of birth control and reasserted that priests must remain unmarried and celibate—his charisma came across well on television. He became the "traveling pope," trotting the globe as a goodwill ambassador for the church, drawing huge crowds to his open-air masses. Church attendance and seminary enrollments usually increased after his visit to a particular country. People around the world—Catholic, Protestant, or other—were enchanted by his warmth and humor. During John Paul's first visit to the United States, for example, he conducted an outdoor mass at Living History Farms, just outside Des Moines, Iowa. Standing toward the back of the crowd, an Iowa farmer, a Protestant, shook his head in admiration. "You've got a pope," he said, turning to his Roman Catholic neighbor, "who really knows how to pope."

*Chapter 6*

# Preachers, Politicians, and Prodigals

**T**he large central building was ringed by bright colors. It looked like a parking lot filled with cars," wrote *Time* correspondent Donald Neff. "When the plane dipped lower, the cars turned out to be bodies—hundreds of bodies—wearing red dresses, blue T-shirts, green blouses, pink slacks, children's polka-dotted jumpers. Couples with their arms around each other, children holding parents. Nothing moved. Washing hung on the clotheslines. The fields were freshly plowed. Banana trees and grape vines were flourishing. But nothing moved."

The scene was an obscure hamlet called Jonestown, deep in the rain forests of Guyana, a small country on the northern coast of South America. News of the mass murder–suicide at Jonestown, a heavily guarded colony founded by a California-based religious group called the Peoples Temple, stunned the world and prompted a flurry of questions about the dangers of religious charisma. The first Peoples Temple had been founded in 1956 by Jim Jones in Indiana, his home state. He moved the group to Redwood City, California, the following year and later set up branches in Los Angeles and San Francisco. The Peoples Temple became known for its interracial membership and its social-welfare activities, including job training, day-care centers, and nursing homes.

Although Jones was recognized for his humanitarian work, he also grew increasingly authoritative and paranoid. He cast himself as "Dad" to

Hundreds of corpses lay in row after horrifying row in fields at the Jonestown compound in Guyana after the 1978 mass murder/suicide.

his followers and demanded submission, often resorting to physical and sexual abuse, threats, and blackmail. He also demanded that members turn over all their property and income to the Peoples Temple. After a series of newspaper and magazine articles brought these practices to light in 1977, Jones relocated his followers to Jonestown, the agricultural colony that his group had established in 1974. When a contingent of Americans led by U.S. Representative Leo Ryan came to Guyana in November 1978 to investigate charges that some members were being held against their will, Jones's followers gunned down Ryan and four others. Retreating to the Jonestown compound, the remaining Peoples Temple members obeyed Jones's infamous order, issued November 18, 1978, to drink a deadly concoction of purple Kool-Aid laced with potassium cyanide. Armed guards enforced the order before obeying it themselves; Jones himself and some of his lieutenants apparently died of self-inflicted gunshot wounds.

As workers sifted through the carnage of 911 corpses—men, women, and children—shocked Americans worried about the destructive effects of religious charisma. At least since the counterculture of the 1960s, reports had circulated about the seductive power of religious personalities, especially those who preyed on young people and turned them against their families. The abduction of newspaper heiress Patty Hearst by an outlaw group calling itself the Symbionese Liberation Army—and Hearst's eventual cooperation with their activities—called further attention to the phenomenon of "programming," or "brainwashing." Groups such as Scientology, est, and Sun Myung Moon's Unification Church all faced criticism as "cults" as well as scrutiny about their beliefs and practices. None, however, faced questions as profound as those framed in the jungles of Guyana, but the dead could not answer.

Although *Newsweek* had christened 1976 the "year of the evangelical," that designation may have been premature. All three major candidates in the Presidential election of 1980—Jimmy Carter, John B. Anderson, and Ronald Reagan—claimed the mantle of evangelicalism. Carter had established his "born-again" credentials during the 1976 campaign;

Anderson, a Republican turned Independent, had been reared in the Evangelical Free Church of America, a denomination with Scandinavian roots; and Ronald Reagan also tried to speak the evangelical language of personal piety.

With the formation of Jerry Falwell's Moral Majority in 1979 and the organization of politically conservative evangelicals as a voting bloc, it became clear that the Religious Right would become a potent force at the polls. While Moral Majority may have been the most visible eruption of Religious Right impulses, other organizations also fit beneath that umbrella, including the Religious Roundtable, Traditional Values Coalition, Focus on the Family, and Concerned Women for America. One of the defining moments of the 1980 Presidential campaign occurred during the Religious Roundtable's first National Affairs Briefing, a rally of 15,000 conservatives in Dallas, Texas. After several stem-winding speeches by right-wing preachers, Reagan, who had been seated on the dais, walked to the podium and said, "I know this is a nonpartisan gathering, and so I know you can't endorse me, but I . . . want you to know that I endorse you and what you are doing." The crowd rose to its feet and shouted "Amen!," thereby all but ensuring that conservative evangelicals would turn their backs on Carter, a fellow evangelical, in favor of Reagan in the November election.

Changes in the telecommunications industry during the 1970s amplified the power of the television preachers, many of whom doubled as leaders of the Religious Right. In the 1950s and 1960s the major television networks, which controlled most of the stations, insisted—in compliance with the Federal Communications Commission (FCC) requirement that all television stations provide a certain amount of public-service time—that their affiliated local stations could not accept money for religious broadcasts they aired. With few exceptions, these stations looked to so-called mainstream religious groups—Protestants, Catholics, and Jews—to provide this programming. By the 1970s, however, when the FCC allowed local stations to accept money for religious programming and, later, with the expansion of cable television, a host of evangelical preachers eagerly

Ronald Reagan campaigns for the Presidency at Jerry Falwell's (left) Liberty University in October 1980. Pollster Lou Harris believes that Reagan would have lost to incumbent Jimmy Carter by one percentage point without the support of Falwell and other Christian conservatives, many of whom were new voters.

took their messages to the airwaves, buying time at bargain prices late at night or during the programming "ghetto" of Sunday morning.

Just as evangelicals had jumped on radio as a means of spreading their message in the 1920s, so, too, they saw the potential for television, especially when coupled with increasingly sophisticated and computerized direct-mail fund-raising operations. No one exploited the medium to better advantage than a young preacher-businessman named Marion G. "Pat" Robertson. The son of a Democratic senator from Virginia and a graduate of Yale Law School, Robertson discerned a call to the ministry after failing to pass the bar exam. After graduating from seminary in 1959, Robertson considered becoming a pastor and applied to be a missionary in Israel. He mulled over the idea of a ministry in the Bedford-Stuyvesant slums of New York City, but nothing seemed to capture his interest until he heard that a defunct television station was for sale in Portsmouth, Virginia, for $37,000.

Robertson visited the station, climbing through a broken window and scaring away a large rat on the glass-strewn floors. He agreed to buy the station on an installment plan, grandly dubbed it the Christian Broadcasting Network (CBN), and by 1961, the same year he was ordained a Southern Baptist minister by the Freemason Street Baptist

Church in Norfolk, Virginia, Robertson began broadcasting three hours of religious television per night.

Although the local clergy remained wary of the struggling enterprise, the station—featuring Robertson's smooth talk and his chatty preaching—began to catch on with viewers. In 1965 Robertson hired two young Assemblies of God evangelists, Jim and Tammy Faye Bakker, as additional talent. Fund-raising telethons fueled the growth of the station and eventually the network as the tentacles of the Christian Broadcasting Network stretched across the nation. An early telethon solicited 700 donors who would pledge ten dollars a month; in 1966 Robertson named his central program, a talk and entertainment format unabashedly based on the *Tonight Show,* the *700 Club,* and it was syndicated nationally in 1972.

By the 1980s the field of television evangelists, who came to be known as televangelists, was crowded. Preachers such as Jimmy Swaggart, Oral Roberts, Kenneth Copeland, James Robison, Robert Schuller, Falwell, and Robertson became household names, devouring millions of dollars annually in contributions. In 1987 *Time* magazine reported that

With the help of a cameraman, this priest is making it possible for Catholics unable to get to church to participate anyway. He is celebrating a Sunday morning mass that is being broadcast live from a Minnesota television studio.

Swaggart had taken in $142 million the previous year, while Falwell brought in about $84 million and Robertson $183 million.

No televangelists garnered more attention in the mid-1980s, however, than Jim and Tammy Faye Bakker, who had left Robertson's Christian Broadcasting Network to start their own operation in Charlotte, North Carolina. The *PTL Club*—variously known as "Praise the Lord," "People that Love," and, by cynics, "Pass the Loot"—featured both of the Bakkers and became the foundation for the PTL Network, which reported revenues of $129 million in 1986. The network soon moved into state-of-the-art production facilities at Heritage USA, the Bakkers' Christian theme park in Fort Mill, South Carolina, which included a hotel, a campground, a shopping mall, restaurants, condominiums, a water amusement park, and Billy Graham's boyhood home.

Jim and Tammy Faye Bakker careened recklessly along whatever line that remained separating preaching from entertainment. Both could send tears gushing at the drop of a hat—or, more likely, in response to a drop in contributions. Tammy Faye was notorious for her goopy makeup—a popular T-shirt in the mid-1980s showed a massive blot of pastels and the legend "I RAN INTO TAMMY FAYE AT THE MALL"—and Jim was a tireless proponent of the so-called prosperity gospel, the "health-and-wealth" doctrine that God was eager to bestow worldly goods on anyone who contributed generously to God's work (read PTL). "We preach prosperity," Bakker said. "We preach abundant life. Christ wished above all things that we prosper." In his eagerness to raise money for Heritage USA, Bakker offered lifetime vacation accommodations to those who contributed substantial sums of money. That tactic would prove to be his legal undoing when it came to light that he had vastly oversold the time-shares and had no way of fulfilling his obligations.

Bakker's spiritual and moral undoing came in the person of Jessica Hahn, a church secretary from Long Island. On March 19, 1987, Bakker abruptly resigned as chairman of PTL. He spoke of a "hostile force" that was threatening him with blackmail in order to take over his religious empire. It later emerged that the "force" was fellow televangelist Jimmy

Swaggart, who excoriated Bakker as a "pretty boy preacher" and a "cancer" on the Body of Christ. At issue was a 1980 tryst between Bakker and Hahn, which Bakker had attempted to conceal with hush money delivered by one of his aides, Richard Dortch. Bakker tried to save PTL by turning it over to another televangelist, Falwell. Still another televangelist, John Ankerberg, stepped forward with charges that Bakker was bisexual.

The drama was played out in the media—including *Good Morning America, Nightline,* and *Time* and *Newsweek* cover stories. The Bakkers' lifestyle of conspicuous consumption—gold-plated bathroom fixtures, Rolls-Royces, air-conditioned doghouses—soon came to light, along with a salary and bonus package that exceeded a million dollars annually, all the while that PTL and Heritage USA sank deeper and deeper into debt. PTL petitioned for bankruptcy, the Internal Revenue Service launched an investigation, and Bakker was defrocked by the Assemblies of God for sexual misconduct. In December 1988 Bakker was indicted on 24 counts of fraud and conspiracy relating to the financial improprieties surrounding PTL and Heritage USA. He was convicted the following year and initially sentenced to 45 years in prison, a sentence later reduced to 8 years.

Bakker's troubles were only the opening act of the televangelist drama that alternated between comedy and tragedy. Oral Roberts, a pentecostal televangelist from Tulsa, Oklahoma, solemnly told his viewers that God had, in effect, taken him hostage and would call Roberts "home"—take him to heaven—unless God's people ponied up something on the order of $4.5 million. On February 21, 1988, more than 7,000 people jammed into Jimmy Swaggart's Family Life Center in Baton Rouge,

Tammy Faye Bakker's big gold bracelet, enormous diamond ring, and golden shoes reflect the lavish life she led with husband Jim Bakker. Their evangelical television network drew millions of dollars annually in contributions.

Jimmy Swaggart and his cousins, entertainers Jerry Lee Lewis and Mickey Gilley, grew up in Ferriday, Louisiana. Swaggart turned down a record contract in order to become a pentecostal preacher, and his energetic sermons—first as an itinerant evangelist and then on radio and television—made him enormously popular.

Louisiana, to hear him confess his own shortcomings. "I do not plan in any way to whitewash my sin," Swaggart said in the wake of disclosures about having visited a motel room with a prostitute. "I do not call it a mistake, a mendacity. I call it sin." In a soliloquy that was baroque and eloquent at the same time, Swaggart apologized to his wife, his son, and his daughter-in-law. He apologized to the Assemblies of God, "which helped to bring the gospel to my little beleaguered town, when my family was lost without Jesus, this movement and fellowship that girdles the globe, that has been more instrumental in bringing this gospel through the stygian night of darkness to the far-flung hundreds of millions than maybe any effort in the annals of history."

Swaggart apologized, finally, to Jesus, "the one who has saved me and washed me and cleansed me." Swaggart's jaw quivered; rivulets of tears flowed down his cheeks. His eyes turned toward heaven. "I have sinned against you, my Lord, and I would ask that your precious blood would wash and cleanse every stain until it is in the seas of God's forgetfulness, never to be remembered against me anymore." The performance was vintage Swaggart—complete with anguish and tears and self-flagellation—but believers shuddered at the toppling of yet another televangelist, and the media, already in a feeding frenzy in the wake of Bakker's tryst with Jessica Hahn, had a field day lampooning the hypocrisy of the televangelists. Ratings—and contributions—for all the televangelists fell precipitously.

Despite the holier-than-thou attitude of the television preachers, it appeared that they were no different from the society at large in the 1980s, which had its own share of corruption. The Reagan administration, in direct violation of the law, had sold armaments to Iran and used the proceeds to fund anti-communist insurgents in Central America. Unscrupulous investors triggered a savings-and-loan scandal, which festered for most of the decade, costing taxpayers billions of dollars. Other investors gravitated toward "junk bonds," high-interest bonds of questionable legality that became the ticket to either quick wealth or financial ruin (or both). The Reagan government preached the virtues of "trickle-down economics," which provided tax cuts for the wealthy together with the hope that the less affluent might benefit as well. The fictional character Gordon Gekko, played by Michael Douglas in the movie *Wall Street,* captured the ideology of the 1980s when he proclaimed, "Greed is good!"

In this context of self-aggrandizement it was no coincidence that televangelists from Jim Bakker and Kenneth Copeland to Robert Tilton and Frederick Price extolled the virtues of something they called "prosperity theology." Simply put, prosperity theology, also known as "name it and claim it," guaranteed that Jesus would not only save your soul and, perhaps, mend your marriage, but he would also find ways to augment your bank account and get you a vacation home and that little red sports car you'd been coveting. The appeals were hardly subtle: Give your money to God—specifically, to whichever preacher was making the pitch—and God will make you financially prosperous.

Not everyone agreed. Many churches and synagogues saw the faces of poverty everywhere around them—on street corners, in soup kitchens, in homeless shelters and rehabilitation centers. Massive governmental cuts in social services in the 1980s (in an effort to help compensate for the tax breaks skewed toward the wealthy) heaped hardship on many Americans, and religious organizations stepped into the breach. In so doing they were reclaiming, though reluctantly, the role they had played a century earlier—running soup kitchens and employment bureaus and otherwise assisting the urban poor—until the massive social problems of the Great Depression overwhelmed them and they were forced to cede those duties to the government.

In one of the most remarkable religious mobilizations of the 20th century, people of faith in the 1980s organized relief efforts on behalf of

## Doonesbury

BY GARRY TRUDEAU

In this 1984 Doonesbury strip, journalist Rick Redfern stands in a soup kitchen line with Alice, a homeless person, and a man who "used to be a human rights analyst for the Carter administration." Budget cuts for social programs during the Reagan Presidency (1981–89) prompted many churches to open such soup kitchens and homeless shelters.

those less fortunate. They turned church basements into soup kitchens and homeless shelters. They also protested federal policies, which placed a higher priority on protecting capital gains and building "Star Wars" weapons systems than on feeding the hungry. For the most part these voices of dissent came from leaders of Roman Catholicism and mainline Protestantism, but others protested as well. People like Jim Wallis of Sojourners, a Christian community located in the ghetto of Washington, D.C., and Ronald Sider of Evangelicals for Social Action represented the political left wing of evangelicalism; while they generally shared the same theology with leaders of the Religious Right, their interpretation of the Bible led them to advocate more liberal political positions.

The approach of the 1988 Presidential campaign represented a challenge for the Religious Right. Although Ronald Reagan had spoken their language and had even appointed a few religious conservatives to positions in his administration, he had failed to prosecute their agenda as vigorously as they hoped he would. Abortion, the rallying issue for the Religious Right, was still legal, despite Reagan's promises to outlaw it; audible prayers, which they supported, were still banned in public school classrooms.

Several Republicans sought the blessing of the Religious Right, but one candidate in particular believed he could use the support of politically conservative evangelicals as a springboard to the nomination. On September 17, 1986, Pat Robertson capitalized on his media exposure, which had been enhanced by CBN's use of satellite technology, and announced that he would become a candidate for the Republican Presidential nomination if he could obtain 3 million signatures of support. Less than a year later he declared his candidacy on a far-right political platform. He took a leave from CBN, resigned his Southern Baptist ordination in September 1987, and studiously billed himself as a broadcasting executive, bristling when the media referred to him as a televangelist. Robertson's attempts to distance himself from his past were not always successful, however. Investigative reporters, for instance, found a tape of a 1985 broadcast of the *700 Club,* when Robertson ordered Hurricane Gloria to change course. "In the name of Jesus," he prayed, "we command you to stop where you are and head northeast, away from land, and away from harm. In the name of Jesus of Nazareth, we command it."

Despite these revelations and with the concerted efforts of politically conservative evangelicals at the grassroots, Robertson won a straw poll in Michigan and finished second to Bob Dole and ahead of George Bush, the eventual nominee, in the Iowa precinct caucuses. "It's almost, like we say, you've got to give God the credit," Robertson declared once the caucus results were in. "Satan has controlled politics for too long," a Robertson supporter remarked to a friend. In the face of increased scrutiny, however, Robertson faltered the following week in New Hampshire and eventually dropped out of the race, but his candidacy lured more evangelicals into the political arena. "Robertson brought out of the pew and into the process tens of thousands of new people, many of whom are still involved," anti-abortion activist Randall Terry said in 1991. "Their full impact will not be felt until the 1996 election, the 2000 election, 2004."

In January 1989, at the inaugural festivities for Bush, Robertson met a young political operative, Ralph Reed. Robertson solicited ideas for transforming the grassroots organizations he had assembled during his campaign into a political lobby for conservative evangelicals. Reed's long memorandum in response provided the blueprint for the Christian Coalition, which was formed later that same year. Robertson, as president of the organization (Reed was tapped as executive director), became a major force in American politics and especially within the Republican

In autumn 1989, these marchers in Tallahassee, Florida, protested the movement to make abortion illegal. Although evangelicals had fought for women's rights in the 19th century, by the end of the 20th the Religious Right, a coalition mainly of politically conservative evangelicals, opposed feminist ideals, especially the right of access to abortion.

party. With his embrace of such ideologies as Christian Reconstructionism, which seeks to replace American civil and criminal codes with the laws of Moses and ancient Israel, including "an eye for an eye, a tooth for a tooth," Robertson was often accused of wanting to collapse the First Amendment distinction between church and state. His excoriations of abortion, political liberals, feminists, and homosexuals earned him the label of intolerant, although such denunciations only served to endear him to many politically conservative evangelicals.

For the better part of three decades the most enduring symbol of the cold war was the Berlin Wall, a tangle of concrete, mines, barbed wire, and armed guards constructed hurriedly by the Communists in 1961 to stanch the flow of East Germans fleeing to freedom in the West. President John F. Kennedy had endeared himself to Germans with his famous *"Ich bin ein Berliner"* (I am a Berliner) speech at the wall, and when Reagan visited there in 1987 he issued a direct challenge to Mikhail Gorbachev, the Soviet president and head of what Reagan once called the "Evil Empire": "Mr. Gorbachev, tear down this wall!" By that time Communism itself was wheezing, crushed beneath the weight of its own failures, and the destruction of the wall itself in November 1989 represented its death rasp.

For nearly three-quarters of a century, since the Bolshevik Revolution of 1917, Americans more often than not had defined themselves in opposition to Communism. America stood for goodness and truth, freedom and righteousness, whereas Communism represented repression, tyranny, and atheism. These cold-war assumptions had dictated everything from military spending to churchgoing. The collapse of the Berlin Wall and the toppling of the Soviet empire may have ushered in what George Bush called the "New World Order," but it also robbed Americans of their most durable adversary. The decade ahead would be marked by an almost desperate casting about for new enemies. Economic and energy considerations suggested the Japanese or the Arabs for a time, but many Americans ultimately decided that enemies lurked closer to home—immigrants, homosexuals, and those they identified as enemies of all religion: "secular humanists."

*Chapter 7*

# Religion for the New Millennium

f the New York World's Fair of 1964–65 symbolized Americans' unalloyed confidence in science and technology, the *Challenger* disaster arguably brought an end to that era of confidence. On the morning of January 28, 1986, a scant 73 seconds into its flight, the space shuttle *Challenger* exploded above the Atlantic Ocean, killing all seven crew members, including Christa McAuliffe, a social studies teacher from Concord, New Hampshire. Americans were transfixed as television played the tape again and again, searing the terrible beauty of that moment—the plumes of white smoke against an azure sky—onto the national consciousness of an entire generation.

Just as Black Thursday in 1929, D-day in 1944, and John Kennedy's assassination in 1963 had been defining moments for previous generations, the *Challenger* disaster—it was referred to almost universally as the "*Challenger* disaster," not "mishap" or "accident"—prompted questions about America's competence, its place in the world, and its reliance on technology, which might itself prove unreliable. Science, technology, and the information age may have made Americans' lives easier at some level—electric can openers and garage-door openers, microwave ovens and personal computers—but they were powerless to impart information on how to live, how to imbue everyday lives with meaning.

Despite the predictions of social scientists, who had warned for more than a century that as any society modernizes and industrializes religion would be pushed to the margins, Americans clung stubbornly to faith at the end of the 20th century. Nationwide membership in the Ethical Culture Society, a secular organization founded in the 19th century to promote good works without religion, to cite one example, fell below 3,000 by the end of the 20th century. More than 90 percent of Americans, on the other hand, professed a belief in God or a supreme being, a figure that had stayed constant since the advent of polling after World War II.

Americans remained religious, but the varieties of religious expression remained anything but constant, and the complexion of America itself was changing. In 1965, amendments to the Immigration and Nationality Act had ended quotas based on nationality, giving rise to major changes in the patterns of immigration to the United States. The number of immigrants from Canada and Europe dropped, whereas immigration from Asia and the West Indies grew dramatically.

Buddhists from Southeast Asia, Sikhs, Jains, and Hindus from South Asia, and Muslims from the Middle East brought their religions with them to the New World and, in so doing, reshaped the religious landscape of America. Sikh *gurdwárás* (temples), Buddhist and Hindu temples, Shinto shrines, and Muslim mosques cropped up alongside of churches, synagogues, and Mormon temples. Vodou and Santería shrines became commonplace in certain neighborhoods of Miami, New Orleans, and New York City, but the patterns of migration ensured that these changes in American religious life would not be confined to urban areas. The oldest mosque in continuous use in the United States, for example, is in Cedar Rapids, Iowa, and one of the major communities of Hare Krishnas, New Vrindavan, lies just outside of Moundsville, West Virginia.

The arrival of these immigrants had other effects. Clergy councils from small towns to big cities faced the prospect of expanding their ranks beyond Protestant ministers, Catholic priests, and Jewish rabbis to include Muslim imams. Many of these councils then mobilized to resist the stereotypical equation of Muslims with terrorism, although the terrorist bomb that ripped through the parking garage of the World Trade Center in lower Manhattan on February 26, 1993, made that task more difficult, especially when the act was traced to Omar Abdel-Rahman, an

Islamic sheik and leader of a radical Muslim group.

Americans greeted new immigrants with attitudes ranging from hostility to indifference to enthusiasm. Tibetan Buddhism, for instance, became popular among various celebrities and Hollywood actors, and the movement's leader, the Dalai Lama, became something of a celebrity himself. Some Americans identified themselves as "Jew-Boos," those who readily combined Jewish ethnicity with Buddhist identity, and Robert A. F. Thurman, one of the Dalai Lama's most devoted acolytes and himself a Tibetan monk, maneuvered to secure an academic appointment at Columbia University, which he used as a platform to attain higher visibility for Tibetan Buddhism.

These Buddhist families have just celebrated the *hatsumairi,* or infant presentation, ceremony. Reverend T. Kenjitsu Nakagaki (background), leader of the New York Buddhist Church, presided.

The resurgence of interest in Asian religions comported well with the fascination with New Age spirituality, a kind of spiritual smorgasbord that encompassed everything from astrology to Zen, various massage therapies, and (for some) belief in extraterrestrials. New Age became all the rage in the 1980s and 1990s. According to a 1987 survey, 67 percent of American adults read astrology reports, and 36 percent believed the reports were scientific. The survey indicated that 42 percent said they had made contact with the spirit of someone who had died; 30 million Americans believed in reincarnation. Nancy Reagan regularly consulted with an astrologer before finalizing her husband's White House schedule. Actress Shirley MacLaine published several best-selling books on New Age spirituality, and NBC aired a situation comedy featuring an alien named "Alf" (Alternative Life Form) from the planet Melmac. New Age music, a kind of dreamy jazz that provided the sensation of drowning in a sea of marzipan, became so popular that the Grammy Awards gave it a special category.

Americans incorporated hitherto "exotic" practices into their daily lives—yoga, tai chi, qi gong, shiatsu massage, all of which combined Eastern spirituality with some sort of physical activity—and saw no contradiction between an adherence to orthodox Christianity or Judaism and New Age practices. Many wore crystals, which were thought to have mysterious healing and spiritual powers, around their necks and worried about their *chakras,* the "energy points" in their bodies. A number of New Agers claimed to be able to "channel," to communicate with, ancient authorities, to speak their words of guidance and warning to a modern age that seemed so bereft of wisdom. Each "channeler" had his or her own character: the archangel Gabriel; Mafu; Zoosh; Soli, an "off-planet being"; or Ramtha, a 35,000-year-old denizen of Atlantis, channeled by J. Z. Knight, an ex-housewife from Yelm, Washington.

In August 1987, 20,000 people participated in a "harmonic convergence," a simultaneous New Age meditation at "sacred sites" from Central Park in New York City to Mount Shasta, California. The New Age had much in common with the environmental movement, believing that the Earth itself was sacred. Such places as Mount Shasta, Boulder, Colorado, Santa Fe, New Mexico, and Sedona, Arizona, became hives of New Age activity. An alternative newspaper in Santa Fe, for example, included advertisements for everything from massage to past-lives counseling (for those who believe in reincarnation and have lived previous lives) and Native American purification ceremonies. New Agers believed that Sedona lay at the intersection of four lines of spiritual energy located deep within the earth, an auspicious circumstance, and people in Sedona talked about the visit of extraterrestrials as casually as New Yorkers discussed traffic on the Gowanus Expressway.

The omnivorous New Age movement sought to appropriate Native American traditions and practices alongside of its other conquests. While the sight of white middle-aged devotees sweating through a purification ceremony merely amused some Native Americans, others regarded them as interlopers and as yet another example of white cultural imperialism. In 1970 an act of Congress had finally restored Taos Blue Lake to the

# Pueblos Make Their Case for Taos Blue Lake

The Taos Pueblos of New Mexico honor Paul Bernal with the presentation of a deerskin and a drum for his leadership in helping his people to retrieve sacred lands, including Blue Lake, from the United States government.

*In 1906 the U.S. Forest Service seized Blue Lake, a sacred site for the Taos Pueblos of northern New Mexico, to include it in Kit Carson National Forest. After decades of fighting to reverse the action, which they considered an infringement on their religious freedom, a delegation of Taos Pueblos appeared before Congress in 1970 to make their case for returning the watershed to the Pueblos. The following year Congress restored the Taos Blue Lake region to the Pueblos. Taos Pueblos testified the following before Congress.*

The entire watershed is permeated with holy places and shrines used regularly by our Indian people; there is no place that does not have religious significance to us. Each of the peaks or valleys, or lakes, springs, and streams has a time in our religious calendar when homage in one form or another must be given, or plants that we have studied and used for centuries gathered, or rituals performed. Our religious leaders and societies go regularly to perform these duties in accordance with this yearly calendar throughout the area. They also supervise, for a period of 18 months, the preparation of our sons for manhood. . . .

Taos Pueblo has used and occupied the watersheds of the Rio Pueblo and Rio Lucero for 700 years or more. We have always practiced conservation of those watersheds; they yield clear water today because of our long-standing care. Today it is more important than ever that the natural conditions of those watersheds be preserved as the source of pure water in those streams.

Pueblos, after a fight that lasted the better part of seven decades, and Native Americans, after the occupation of Wounded Knee, South Dakota, in 1973, had begun to reclaim their religious traditions at powwows, in kivas, or sweat lodges, or beneath the sacred sky. The Supreme Court, however, dealt another blow to Native Americans in 1990 when it ruled that there was no constitutional right to chew the hallucinogenic drug peyote in Native American religious practices. "We have never held that an individual's religious beliefs excuse him from compliance with an otherwise valid law prohibiting conduct that the state is free to regulate," the majority ruled in a 6-to-3 decision.

Native Americans quickly protested the ruling, pointing out that use of peyote in their religious ceremonies predated the Constitution. Religious groups and newspaper editorial pages across the country also decried the decision as a violation of the First Amendment guarantee of free exercise of religion. The *Des Moines Register,* for example, called the decision "awful" and characterized the Court's action as "a gratuitous swipe at its historic deference to religious freedom." A broad spectrum of religious leaders appealed to Congress for redress; Congress responded with the Religious Freedom Restoration Act, which argued that "governments should not substantially burden religious exercise without compelling justification." President Bill Clinton signed the bill into law on November 16, 1993, but the Supreme Court continued the tug-of-war by declaring the measure invalid in 1997, an indication to many of the fragility of First Amendment freedoms.

Other minorities faced threats as well, including threats from a motley collection of white supremacist "hate groups" bunched beneath the umbrella of Christian Identity, a reference to their belief that white Christians are God's chosen people. The ideologies driving these groups differed, but they generally directed their invectives against Jews, homosexuals, and minorities, especially African Americans. Some unabashedly claimed the legacy of Nazism, many were survivalists of various sorts (those who want to live without depending on the economic system— even grocery stores—for their existence), and almost all harbored deep

A mourner from Oklahoma decorates a roadside cross in memory of one of the agents from the Bureau of Alcohol, Tobacco, and Firearms who died in the U.S. government siege of David Koresh's Branch Davidian compound at Waco, Texas, in April 1993.

suspicions of government. Inevitably, these groups clashed with federal officials, as when Randy Weaver, a survivalist wanted on weapons charges, faced off against law-enforcement officers in Ruby Ridge, Idaho; such confrontations stoked the paranoia and the hatred of Christian Identity groups toward the government.

Another confrontation, just outside of Waco, Texas, pitted the Bureau of Alcohol, Tobacco, and Firearms against a heavily armed colony of Branch Davidians, a religious sect led by David Koresh, who believed he was a messiah. After a standoff lasting 51 days and persistent reports about child abuse within the group, federal agents finally moved against the compound on the morning of April 19, 1993. The buildings erupted in a conflagration that killed at least 80 Branch Davidians, including Koresh. The most disastrous reprisal against the federal government occurred two years later to the day, on April 19, 1995, when a young vigilante named Timothy McVeigh and an unknown number of accomplices conspired to bomb the Alfred P. Murrah Federal Building in Oklahoma City, Oklahoma, leaving 168 dead, including 19 children. The incident, the most devastating terrorist act on American soil, traumatized the nation, but it also cast light into some of the darker corners of American religious life and exposed Identity and survivalist groups to public scrutiny and scorn.

Three decades after the Civil Rights Act black Americans were still struggling for their Constitutional rights against the hoary vestiges of racism. California and other states sought to do away with affirmative action, a system of racial quotas that had helped minorities aspire to equal opportunity in education and employment. Dozens of African-American churches across the South, from Virginia to Louisiana, mysteriously caught fire in the 1990s, prompting a Justice Department official to call it "an epidemic of terror." The targeting of churches may have been significant because of the role that churches had played in the civil-rights movement. Noting that the terrorists were not burning African-American businesses, Randolph Scott-McLaughlin of the Center for Constitutional Rights said: "They're burning down black churches. It's like they're burning a cross in my front yard. They're burning symbols of resistance and community and hope and refuge."

Congregants hold hands as they gather to dedicate the Heartland Chapel in July 1995, in memory of the victims of the bombing of the Alfred P. Murrah Federal Building in Oklahoma City, Oklahoma. The chapel is attached to a church that was damaged in the bombing. The wide-open space behind the flag is where the federal office building once stood.

Amid the embers of hate and destruction, however, some religious leaders saw signs of hope, even reconciliation. The arson of African-American houses of worship provoked ringing denunciations from Americans in all walks of life. "These attacks against African-American churches and other houses of worship are an affront to our most basic beliefs of religious liberty and racial tolerance," Bill Clinton said on July 2, 1996. "They pose a challenge to our entire nation." The Clinton administration established the National Church Arson Task Force, and Congress passed the Church Arson Prevention Act; within six months, nearly 150 people had been arrested. Individuals, congregations, corporations, even the players in the National Football League provided money for the rebuilding of churches; college students volunteered their labor, and the churches rose again. "We can never define ourselves as Americans by saying we are so good because we are not the other guy," Clinton remarked to a gathering of the Congressional Black Caucus on September 14, 1996, in response to the church burnings. "The other guys are us, too. We are all Americans."

Part of the rose window over the door of Grace Chapel Ministries of St. Louis, Missouri, exploded in a fire started by arsonists in March 1996. The African-American church had to be boarded up after this racist act of destruction.

Another challenge to racism in the 1990s came from an improbable source. On March 20, 1990, Bill McCartney, head football coach at the University of Colorado, and his friend Dave Wardell were traveling to a meeting of the Fellowship of Christian Athletes, in Pueblo, Colorado. In the course of their conversation, they came upon the idea of filling Colorado's Folsom Stadium with men dedicated to the notion of Christian devotion and discipline. This vision spread to a cohort of 72 men, who engaged in fasting and prayer in support of the notion.

More than 4,000 men showed up for the first gathering, and by July 1993 McCartney's original vision had been fulfilled. Fifty thousand men piled into Folsom Stadium for singing, hugging, and exhortations to be good and faithful husbands, fathers, and churchgoers. McCartney also insisted that his overwhelmingly white, middle-class audience bridge the barriers of racial hatred. By 1996 the organization, Promise Keepers, had an annual budget in excess of $115 million and offices in 32 states and provinces throughout North America. In 1995 more than 1 million men attended 22 rallies at sports stadiums across the country, and on October 4, 1997, Promise Keepers conducted a mass rally, called "Stand in the Gap: A Sacred Assembly of Men," on the Mall in Washington, D.C.

Promise Keepers was merely the latest manifestation of a phenomenon called muscular Christianity, a series of initiatives to make Christianity more attractive to men. At least since the late 17th century women have outnumbered men in religious adherence, a circumstance that has prompted these periodic attempts to lure men back to the churches. The Awakening of 1857–58, for instance, also known as the Businessman's Revival, appealed to men in the workplace with weekday noontime prayer meetings. At the turn of the 20th century Billy Sunday, formerly a baseball player for the Chicago White Stockings, cajoled the men in his audiences to "hit the sawdust trail" and give their lives to Jesus.

"Many think a Christian has to be a sort of dishrag proposition, a wishy-washy, sissified sort of galoot that lets everybody make a doormat out of him," Sunday intoned. "Let me tell you the manliest man is the man who will acknowledge Jesus Christ." A few years later, at about the same time that Charles Sheldon's novel *In His Steps* portrayed Jesus as an astute businessman, an organization called the Men and Religion Forward Movement summoned men back to the churches with the slogan "More Men for Religion, More Religion for Men." The campaign held rallies in places like Carnegie Hall, rented billboards on Times Square, and placed display ads in the sports sections of newspapers.

Ever since the New Testament, Christianity has employed athletic metaphors to talk about the Christian life. St. Paul talked about the importance of running the race, and such organizations as the YMCA used sports as a means to lure men away from the temptations of the streets. In 1902 John Scudder, a Congregational minister in New York City, opened a

A Christian man opens his arms in prayer in the midst of thousands of fellow Promise Keepers at a rally at Robert F. Kennedy Stadium in Washington, D.C. Movement founder Bill McCartney, the University of Colorado football coach, urged American men to be good and faithful husbands, fathers, and churchgoers.

gymnasium at his church in order to teach boys to box and thereby "inculcate virtues of highest moral value" because "manly sparring tends toward Christian growth." In the 1950s and 1960s James C. Hefley, an evangelical author, published edifying biographical sketches of professional athletes who professed to be Christians: Bobby Richardson, Dave Wickersham, Bill Glass, Al Worthington, among many others. A number of organizations emphasized the connection between sports and Christianity: Athletes in Action, the Fellowship of Christian Athletes, and Power Team for Christ, a weight-lifting troupe that traveled to various venues and interspersed evangelistic testimonies with spectacular feats of strength.

It should have come as no surprise, then, that Promise Keepers, the muscular Christianity of the 1990s, took on the trappings of athleticism. McCartney, founder of Promise Keepers, was a highly successful football coach who led the Colorado Buffaloes from obscurity to national rankings and the Associated Press National Championship in 1990. McCartney's rhetoric drew on athletic imagery; Promise Keepers rallies and publications most often featured athletes; and the gatherings themselves took place in sports arenas. Like evangelicals throughout American history before him, McCartney had found a way to speak the idiom of American men of a particular time.

Promise Keepers was the decade's Rorschach test, the exercise in which observers try to make sense of a random ink blot. Analysts of every stripe—and there was no shortage of analysts—saw in this men's mass movement almost anything, or at least whatever they wanted to see. Apologists regarded it as a religious revival, a moment of racial healing, and an important movement reminding men of their God-given responsibilities. Detractors saw Promise Keepers as frontal assault on homosexuality and feminism and as a tool of the Religious Right. Historians saw precedents in the ritual tradition of ancient Israel, in the religious awakenings of the 18th and 19th centuries, and in the camp meetings of the antebellum frontier. Marxists pointed to the movement's appeal to middle-class sensibilities and its commercialism, as evident in T-shirts, audiocassettes, books, and trinkets. Politically minded analysts identified Promise Keepers as yet another front in the so-called culture wars of the 1990s. Cultural historians cited precedents in fraternal orders, such as the Masons or the Elks Club, with the stadium replacing lodge rooms as a place to reaffirm one's masculinity.

Amid all the analysis, the detractors generally failed to notice that McCartney was delivering a message that few others dared to articulate. In an era of rampant divorce, physical abuse of spouses (as illustrated in the O. J. Simpson case), and general male irresponsibility, McCartney enjoined men to be responsible husbands, fathers, and churchgoers. Although Promise Keepers offended feminists with its patriarchalism (men were told to return home and take charge of their households), it sought to mollify women by emphasizing the soft-breasted male, a man who was not afraid to admit his mistakes, to show his vulnerability, even to cry.

As with most eruptions of religious enthusiasm and as with previous incarnations of muscular Christianity, Promise Keepers faded almost as quickly as it had arisen. Within months of the Stand in the Gap rally Promise Keepers announced that it would lay off most of its staff and rely on volunteer labor, although a modest infusion of contributions kept the organization alive, if only on life support.

With the approach of the year 2000 Americans were infected with millennial fever. An automobile company named one of its models Millenia, and a hotel in lower Manhattan took the name "Millenium" (although it is worth pointing out that both versions were misspelled: *millennium* has a double "n"). Lubavitch Hasidic Jews, those who practiced a strict form of Orthodoxy, believed that their rebbe, Menachem Schneerson, was the long-awaited messiah foretold by the Hebrew prophets, and his death in 1994 did little to dampen their ardor.

Many evangelical Christians, long preoccupied with the end of time because of their literal interpretation of the book of Revelation, detected a confluence between the calendar and their expectations of the return of Jesus. Most, however, were loath to make specific predictions because such claims in the past had proved false. In the early 1840s, for example, a farmer and biblical interpreter from Low Hampton, New York, calculated that Jesus would return sometime in 1843 or 1844. William Miller tirelessly publicized his predictions, and by the time the deadline arrived,

Lubavitcher Rabbi Menachem Schneerson crowns a new Torah, a scroll that contains the first five books of the bible, at a Lubavitch Center ceremony.

October 22, 1844, more than fifty thousand people had expressed sympathy for his teachings; so frenzied was some of the rhetoric about the imminent Second Coming that Horace Greeley felt obliged to publish a special edition of the *New-York Tribune* to refute Miller's teachings.

Other religious groups in American history have fashioned their beliefs around the conviction that human history would soon come to an end. Joseph Smith taught (and Mormons still believe) that the center stake of Zion, the heavenly city, will be in Jackson County, Missouri. On Good Friday, 1878, Charles Taze Russell and a handful of his followers gathered on the Sixth Street Bridge in Pittsburgh to await their ascension into heaven; Russell's present-day followers, the Jehovah's Witnesses, still carry the message of apocalyptic judgment throughout the world.

Evocations of the end of time permeated countless sermons, motion pictures, and books. Billy Graham, for instance, often talked about the return of Jesus, and he wrote several books about the apocalypse predicted in the Bible. With the approach of 2000 and the turn of the millennium, moreover, speculation about the apocalypse reached a fever pitch. Clyde Lott, a fundamentalist and a cattle breeder from Mississippi, undertook a project to breed a Red Angus that would be available for the restoration of animal sacrifice when the Jewish Temple was rebuilt in Jerusalem. Such an animal would conform to the specifications spelled out in the book of Numbers in the Hebrew Bible: "Speak unto the children of Israel," the Lord said, "that they bring thee a red heifer without spot, wherein is no blemish, and upon which never came a yoke." The rebuilding of the Temple, of course, might indeed bring on the end of the world because the Temple Mount in Jerusalem already had a tenant, the Islamic Dome of the Rock, and any move by American fundamentalists or Jewish zealots to raze the Muslim holy place to make room for the Jewish Temple would certainly provoke a cataclysmic response.

Some evangelicals at the end of the second millennium even speculated about the identity of the Antichrist, a charismatic, devious person, according to the book of Revelation, who will lead many away from the truth. While Protestant speculation through the centuries had often centered on the pope (because of anti-Catholic bias), evangelicals in the 20th

# Religion in a Pluralistic Society

*Mario Cuomo, a devout Roman Catholic and governor of New York from 1983 to 1995, was an eloquent spokesman for the Democratic party and for his faith, even though his generally liberal political views, especially on birth control and abortion, sometimes placed him at odds with more conservative Catholic bishops. On September 13, 1984, during the heat of the Presidential campaign and during the height of the influence of the Religious Right, Cuomo spoke at the University of Notre Dame about the responsibilities of an elected official in a pluralistic society.*

[T]he Catholic who holds political office in a pluralistic democracy—who is elected to serve Jews and Moslems, atheists and Protestants, as well as Catholics—bears special responsibility. He or she undertakes to help create conditions under which *all* can live with a maximum of dignity and with a reasonable degree of freedom; where everyone who chooses may hold beliefs different from specifically Catholic ones—sometimes contradictory to them; where the laws protect people's right to divorce, to use birth control, and even to choose an abortion.

In fact, Catholic public officials take an oath to preserve the Constitution that guarantees this freedom. And they do so gladly. Not because they love what others do with their freedom, but because they realize that in guaranteeing freedom for all, they guarantee *our* right to be Catholics; *our* right to pray, to use the sacraments, to refuse birth control devices, to reject abortion, not to divorce and remarry if we believe it to be wrong.

The Catholic public official lives the political truth most Catholics, throughout most of American history, have accepted and insisted on: the truth that to assure our freedom we must allow others the same freedom, even if occasionally it produces conduct by them that we would hold to be sinful.

I protect my right to be a Catholic by preserving your right to believe as a Jew, a Protestant, a nonbeliever, or an anything else you choose. We know that the price of seeking to force our beliefs on others is that they might someday force theirs on us. This freedom is the fundamental strength of our unique experiment in government.

A volunteer from an Islamic group based in Brooklyn, New York, distributes food and clothing from a van to the homeless in mid-Manhattan.

century also suggested other candidates, ranging from Adolf Hitler to Mikhail Gorbachev to Ronald Wilson Reagan, who had six letters in each of his three names, corresponding to 666, the Mark of the Beast. In a missive widely distributed over the Internet, someone asserted that if you convert the letters of his name to ASCII numbers, Bill Gates (3rd) totals 666. The posting also included the corroborating information that "Windows 95," when parsed into ASCII numbers, also equals 666.

The mention of Gates, head of Microsoft and the world's wealthiest man, suggests another reason for anxiety as the year 2000 approached. The so-called Y2K computer bug, caused by the inability of the internal clocks in some computers to recognize the digits 00 as the year 2000 rather than 1900, led many Americans to fear all manner of calamities (including the loss of their retirement savings) at the stroke of midnight, December 31, 1999. Many became survivalists, buying generators and stockpiling provisions, even relocating to the wilderness, while others suggested that the Y2K crisis might be part of a larger apocalypse that would unfold at the turn of the millennium, thereby fulfilling biblical prophecies about the end of time.

As Americans faced a new millennium they could look back on a century full of contradictions. The 1900s witnessed the granting of legal equality to all Americans, regardless of religion, skin color, gender, or sexual orientation, even though the reality often fell short of that ideal. While some Americans finally attained full rights of citizenship, through the Civil Rights Act of 1964, for example, the 20th century was arguably the genocidal century—two World Wars, the Holocaust, the dropping of the atomic bomb on Hiroshima, persistent ethnic conflict in Northern Ireland, the Middle East, and Bosnia—all providing ample evidence of human depravity. The technological revolution transported Americans from horse-and-buggy days to space travel, with several stops on the moon, but technology also proved destructive and unreliable, witness the environmental threat of industrialization and the *Challenger* disaster of 1986.

The one constant, however, amid massive cultural changes, was that Americans remained incurably religious, however variously they defined their religious lives, be it Protestant or Hindu, Jewish or New Age, Mormon, Buddhist, or Roman Catholic—or some wildly eclectic combination. Despite industrialization, modernization, even secularization, Americans clung stubbornly to religion and spirituality. This was the legacy they carried into the 21st century.

# *Chronology*

**1901**
Pentecostal revival, including speaking in tongues, breaks out at Bethel Bible College in Topeka, Kansas, on the first day of the new century

**1904**
North American Shinto Church organized in San Francisco (later moves to Los Angeles)

**1906**
San Francisco Vedanta Society builds first Hindu temple in North America

U.S. Forest Service annexes the Taos Blue Lake region, a sacred site to the Pueblos of northern New Mexico

**1906–09**
Pentecostal revival spreads to Los Angeles and becomes known as the Azusa Street Revival

**1907**
Walter Rauschenbusch, theologian at Rochester Theological Seminary and former pastor in the Hell's Kitchen area of Manhattan, publishes *Christianity and the Social Crisis,* the manifesto of the Social Gospel movement

**1908**
Vatican declares that the United States is no longer missionary territory

**1910–15**
*The Fundamentals,* a series of pamphlets arguing for a return to conservative Protestant theology, is published

**1911**
Catholic Foreign Missionary Society of America founded in Maryknoll, New York

**1912**
Pacific Coast Khalsa Diwan Society establishes first North American Sikh *gurdwara* (temple) in Holt, California

**1915**
Leo Frank, a Jew accused of the murder of Mary Phagan, is lynched by a mob on August 16 after the Georgia governor commutes his death penalty to life in prison

William J. Simmons, a former Methodist minister, revives the Ku Klux Klan

**1916**
President Woodrow Wilson appoints Louis Brandeis, a Jew, to the U.S. Supreme Court

**1922**
Aimee Semple McPherson, a pentecostal, becomes the first woman to preach a sermon over the radio

**1925**
Scopes trial in Dayton, Tennessee, dramatizes the debate between Darwinism and the Genesis account of creation

Presbyterians, Methodists, and Congregationalists unite to form United Church of Canada

**1926**

Synagogue Council of America, an organization of Conservative Jews, is established in New York City on November 9

Charles E. Coughlin, a Roman Catholic priest, begins his radio program, which remains on the air until 1940

**1929**

In one of the major skirmishes of the fundamentalist-modernist controversy, Presbyterian theologian J. Gresham Machen leaves Princeton Theological Seminary to form Westminster Theological Seminary in Philadelphia

**1930**

Catholic Youth Organization (CYO) founded in Chicago

**1932**

*Re-Thinking Missions,* the summary of a study of Protestant missions, is published; calls for missionary collaboration with other faiths rather than the traditional focus on conversion and cultural conquest

**1933**

The first issue of the *Catholic Worker,* a Christian socialist newspaper, is published in New York City on May 1

**1934**

Mordecai Kaplan publishes *Judaism as a Civilization,* the manifesto of Reconstructionist Judaism

**1944**

Congress passes the GI Bill of Rights, which provides opportunities for the sons of immigrants, especially Catholic immigrants, to attend college after serving in the military

**1948**

Thomas Merton's *Seven Storey Mountain* is published, calling attention to both Catholicism and the contemplative life

**1949**

Protestant leaders in Cleveland form National Council of Churches during a November meeting

**1950**

During his revival "crusade" in Portland, Oregon, evangelist Billy Graham decides to incorporate his ministry, the Billy Graham Evangelistic Association, and to initiate a regular radio broadcast, *The Hour of Decision*

**1954**

Supreme Court's *Brown* v. *Board of Education* decision on May 17 paves the way for the dismantling of segregation

**1955**

Will Herberg of Drew University publishes *Protestant, Catholic, Jew,* providing an intellectual justification for the so-called Judeo-Christian tradition

Montgomery, Alabama, bus boycott begins in December; Martin Luther King, Jr., is chosen to lead the Montgomery Improvement Association

**1956**

Presbyterian Church (USA) allows the ordination of women

**1958**

Dwight D. Eisenhower lays the cornerstone of the Interchurch Center in upper Manhattan on October 12, the same day that a bomb rips through Atlanta's Hebrew Benevolent Society, the city's oldest Reform Jewish congregation

**1959**

Dennis J. Bennett, the rector of St. Mark's Episcopal Church in Van Nuys, California, announces to his parish that he has spoken in tongues, thereby heralding the charismatic movement within the Episcopal Church

**1960**

John F. Kennedy of Massachusetts becomes the first Roman Catholic elected to the U.S. Presidency

**1962–65**

Second Vatican Council in Rome brings profound changes in Roman Catholic teaching; Catholics in America generally embrace the reforms, including the recitation of the mass in the vernacular

**1963**

March on Washington in August calls attention to the need for civil-rights reforms

**1964**

Martin Luther King, Jr., is awarded the Nobel Peace Prize

**1965**

Malcolm X is assassinated while speaking at the Audubon Ballroom in New York City on February 21

The Immigration and Nationality Act ends the quota system for immigration, opening the way for increased immigration from Asia

**1967**

Faculty members from Duquesne University in Pittsburgh attend a pentecostal retreat, triggering the Catholic Charismatic Renewal movement

**1968**

Martin Luther King, Jr., is assassinated in Memphis, Tennessee, on April 4

Pope Paul VI issues *Humanae Vitae,* which affirms that the use of artificial means of birth control violates Catholic church teaching

**1969**

James Forman issues a "Black Manifesto" to the National Council of Churches demanding reparations for slavery

**1970**

An act of Congress returns the sacred Blue Lake to the Taos Pueblos

**1972**

Sally Priesand, a Reform Jew, becomes the first woman ordained as a rabbi

**1973**

A band of Native Americans occupies Wounded Knee, South Dakota, site of the massacre of Sioux by federal troops in 1890, to call attention to the plight American Indians

Tenzin Gyatso, the 14th Dalai Lama, makes his first of many visits to the West; he becomes a kind of goodwill ambassador for Tibetan Buddhism

**1974**

Chogyam Trungpa, a Tibetan Buddhist monk, establishes the Naropa Institute (now Naropa University) in Boulder, Colorado, which becomes the first accredited Buddhist-inspired liberal arts college in America

Eleven female deacons are ordained to the Episcopal priesthood in Philadelphia on July 29

**1976**

Jimmy Carter, a "born-again" evangelical Christian and former Democratic governor of Georgia, wins election to the Presidency

**1978**

Spencer W. Kimball, president of the Church of Jesus Christ of Latter-day Saints, announces on June 9 that men of color can enter the Mormon priesthood

On November 18, members of the Peoples Temple obey their leader's instruction to commit mass suicide in Jonestown, Guyana

**1979**

Jerry Falwell founds Moral Majority, a political organization intended to bring politically conservative evangelicals into the political process

Conservatives (also known as fundamentalists) succeed in electing Adrian Rogers president of the Southern Baptist Convention, initiating what becomes a "takeover" of the denomination

**1980**

Three candidates for President—Jimmy Carter, John B. Anderson, and Ronald Reagan—all claim to be evangelical Christians; the Religious Right throws its support to Reagan, helping to secure his election (as well as his reelection four years later)

**1986**

Elie Wiesel, Holocaust survivor whose life is dedicated to writing and speaking about the Holocaust, wins the Nobel Peace Prize

**1987**

A New Age "harmonic convergence" at sacred sites from New York to California takes place in August

Televangelist Pat Robertson, one of the leaders of the Religious Right, mounts a campaign for the Republican Presidential nomination

**1989**

Pat Robertson and Ralph Reed collaborate to form the Christian Coalition, a lobby group for politically conservative evangelicals

**1993**

Federal officials attack the Branch Davidian compound outside of Waco, Texas, on April 19, killing most of the inhabitants

World's Parliament of Religions, a centennial observance of the first Parliament, meets in Chicago

President Bill Clinton signs the Religious Freedom Restoration Act

**1994**

Rebbe Menachem Schneerson, leader of the Lubavitcher group of Hasidic Jews, dies; most of his followers consider him to be the messiah, and some continue to look for his resurrection

**1997**

Promise Keepers, an organization of evangelical men, hold their "Stand in the Gap" rally in Washington, D.C., on October 4

**1999**

Popular fears about the Y2K "computer bug" and terrorism combine with apocalyptic predictions as December 31 approaches; the transition from 1999 to 2000 takes place virtually without a hitch

# *Further Reading*

## GENERAL

Ahlstrom, Sidney E. *A Religious History of the American People.* New Haven, Conn.: Yale University Press, 1972.

Albanese, Catherine L. *America, Religions, and Religion.* 3rd ed. Belmont, Calif.: Wadsworth, 1999.

Butler, Jon, and Harry S. Stout, eds. *Religion in American History: A Reader.* New York: Oxford University Press, 1997.

Gaustad, Edwin. *A Religious History of America.* Rev. ed. San Francisco: Harper & Row, 1990.

Marty, Martin. *Pilgrims in Their Own Land: 500 Years of Religion in America.* New York: Penguin, 1985.

## BIOGRAPHIES

Arrington, Leonard J. *Adventures of a Church Historian.* Urbana: University of Illinois Press, 1998.

Berrigan, Philip. *Fighting the Lamb's War: Skirmishes with the American Empire: The Autobiography of Philip Berrigan.* Monroe, Me.: Common Courage Press, 1996.

Blumhofer, Edith L. *Aimee Semple McPherson: Everybody's Sister.* Grand Rapids, Mich.: Eerdmans, 1993.

Brown, Karen McCarthy. *Mama Lola: A Vodou Priestess in Brooklyn.* Berkeley: University of California Press, 1991.

Burnham, Kenneth E. *God Comes to America: Father Divine and the Peace Mission Movement.* Boston: Lambeth Press, 1979.

Cunningham, Lawrence. *Thomas Merton and the Monastic Vision.* Grand Rapids, Mich.: Eerdmans, 1999.

Dorset, Lyle W. *Billy Sunday and the Redemption of Urban America.* Grand Rapids, Mich.: Eerdmans, 1991.

Flood, Renee S. *Lost Bird of Wounded Knee: Heroic Spirit of the Lakota.* New York: Scribner, 1995.

Friedman, Maurice S. *Abraham Joshua Heschel and Elie Wiesel: You Are My Witnesses.* New York: Farrar, Straus & Giroux, 1987.

Fox, Richard Wightman. *Reinhold Niebuhr: A Biography.* New York: Pantheon, 1985.

Garrow, David J. *Bearing the Cross: Martin Luther King, Jr., and the Southern Christian Leadership Conference.* New York: Random House, 1986.

George, Carol V. R. *God's Salesman: Norman Vincent Peale and the Power of Positive Thinking.* New York: Oxford University Press, 1993.

Goff, James R., Jr. *Fields White unto Harvest: Charles F. Parham and the Missionary Origins of Pentecostalism.* Fayetteville: University of Arkansas Press, 1988.

Harrell, David Edwin, Jr. *Oral Roberts: An American Life.* Bloomington: Indiana University Press, 1985.

———. *Pat Robertson: A Personal, Religious, and Political Portrait.* San Francisco: Harper & Row, 1987.

Malcolm X, with Alex Haley. *The Autobiography of Malcolm X.* New York: Grove Press, 1964.

Martin, William. *A Prophet with Honor: The Billy Graham Story.* New York: William Morrow, 1991.

Polner, Murray. *Disarmed and Dangerous: The Radical Lives and Times of Daniel and Philip Berrigan.* New York: Basic Books, 1997.

Prothero, Stephen R. *The White Buddhist: The Asian Odyssey of Henry Steel Olcott.* Bloomington: Indiana University Press, 1996.

Rosen, Steven. *A Passage from India: The Life and Times of His Divine Grace A. C. Bhaktivedanta Swami Prabhupada.* New Delhi: Munshiram Manoharlal Publishers, 1992.

Scult, Mel. *Judaism Faces the Twentieth Century: A Biography of Mordecai M. Kaplan.* Detroit: Wayne State University Press, 1993.

Seaman, Ann Rowe. *Swaggart: The Unauthorized Biography of an American Evangelist.* New York: Continuum, 1999.

Tworkov, Helen. *Zen in America: Profiles of Five Teachers and the Search for an American Buddhism.* Rev. ed. New York: Kodansha, 1995.

## RELIGIOUS TRADITIONS AND MOVEMENTS

Alexander, Thomas G. *Mormonism in Transition: A History of the Latter-day Saints, 1890–1930.* Urbana: University of Illinois Press, 1986.

Allen, James B., and Richard Cowan. *Mormonism in the Twentieth Century.* 2nd ed. Provo, Ut.: Brigham Young University Press, 1967.

Ammerman, Nancy. *Baptist Battles: Social Change and Religious Conflict in the Southern Baptist Convention.* New Brunswick, N.J.: Rutgers University Press, 1990.

Balmer, Randall. *Blessed Assurance: A History of Evangelicalism in America.* Boston: Beacon Press, 1999.

———. *Grant Us Courage: Travels Along the Mainline of American Protestantism.* New York: Oxford University Press, 1996.

———. *Mine Eyes Have Seen the Glory: A Journey into the Evangelical Subculture in America.* 3rd ed. New York: Oxford University Press, 2000.

Blumhofer, Edith L. *Restoring the Faith: The Assemblies of God, Pentecostalism, and American Culture.* Urbana: University of Illinois Press, 1993.

Carpenter, Joel A. *Revive Us Again: The Reawakening of American Fundamentalism.* New York: Oxford University Press, 1997.

Chidester, David. *Salvation and Suicide: An Interpretation of Jim Jones, the Peoples Temple, and Jonestown.* Bloomington: Indiana University Press, 1988.

Cox, Harvey. *Fire from Heaven: The Rise of Pentecostal Spirituality and the Reshaping of Religion in the Twenty-First Century.* Reading, Mass.: Addison-Wesley, 1995.

Dinnerstein, Leonard. *Uneasy at Home: Antisemitism and the American Jewish Experience.* New York: Columbia University Press, 1987.

Dolan, Jay P. *The American Catholic Experience: A History from Colonial Times to the Present.* Garden City, N.Y.: Doubleday, 1985.

Fields, Rick. *How the Swans Came to the Lake: A Narrative History of Buddhism in America.* 3rd ed. Boston: Shambhala, 1992.

Freedman, Samuel G. *Upon this Rock: The Miracles of a Black Church.* New York: HarperCollins, 1993.

Gordon-McCutchan, R. C. *The Taos Indians and the Battle for Blue Lake.* Santa Fe, N.M.: Red Crane Books, 1991.

Hutchison, William R. *Errand to the World: American Protestant Thought and Foreign Missions.* Chicago: University of Chicago Press, 1987.

Joselit, Jenna Weissman. *The Wonders of America: Reinventing Jewish Culture, 1880–1950.* New York: Hill & Wang, 1994.

McCauley, Deborah Vansau. *Appalachian Mountain Religion: A History.* Urbana: University of Illinois Press, 1995.

McGreevy, John T. *Parish Boundaries: The Catholic Encounter with Race in the Twentieth-Century Urban North.* Chicago: University of Chicago Press, 1996.

Marsden, George M. *Fundamentalism and American Culture: The Shaping of Twentieth-Century Evangelicalism: 1870–1925.* New York: Oxford University Press, 1980.

Martin, William. *With God on Our Side: The Rise of the Religious Right in America.* New York: Broadway Books, 1996.

Massa, Mark S. *Catholics and American Culture: Fulton Sheen, Dorothy Day, and the Notre Dame Football Team.* New York: Crossroad, 1999.

Miller, Donald E. *Reinventing American Protestantism: Christianity in the New Millennium.* Berkeley: University of California Press, 1997.

Moore, Deborah Dash. *To the Golden Cities: Pursuing the American Dream in Miami and Los Angeles.* New York: Free Press, 1994.

Murphy, Joseph M. *Santería: An African Religion in America.* Boston: Beacon Press, 1980.

Orsi, Robert Anthony. *The Madonna of 115th Street: Faith and Community in Italian Harlem, 1880–1950.* New Haven, Conn.: Yale University Press, 1985.

Ostling, Richard N., and Joan K. Ostling. *Mormon America: The Power and the Promise.* San Francisco: Harper San Francisco, 1999.

Roof, Wade Clark, and William McKinney. *American Mainline Religion: Its Changing Shape and Future.* New Brunswick, N.J.: Rutgers University Press, 1987.

Smith, Paul Chaat. *Like a Hurricane: The Indian Movement from Alcatraz to Wounded Knee.* New York: New Press, 1996.

Tweed, Thomas A. *The American Encounter with Buddhism, 1844–1912: Victorian Culture and the Limits of Dissent.* Bloomington: Indiana University Press, 1992.

———and Stephen Prothero, eds. *Asian Religions in America: A Documentary History.* New York: Oxford University Press, 1999.

———. *Our Lady of the Exile: Diasporic Religion at a Cuban Catholic Shrine in Miami.* New York: Oxford University Press, 1997.

# Index

*References to illustrations and their captions are indicated by page numbers in* **boldface.**

Abortion, 94–97, **110**
African Americans, 56–60, 70–81; and racists, 34–35, 40, 56, 71, 118, 120–**21**; religions, 14, 36–37, 87. *See also* Civil rights
Alcohol, 22, 31, 37
Ali, Noble Drew. *See* Drew, Timothy
American Civil Liberties Union (ACLU), 29
American Protective Association, 12
Anderson, John B., 100–101
Ankerberg, John, 105
Anti-Catholicism, 12, 34–**35,** 37–38, 40, 63–**64, 66,** 126. *See also* Catholics
Anti-Semitism, 20–**21,** 34–**35,** 40, 71, 118. *See also* Jews
Apocalypse, 13, 15, 126, 128
*Apostolic Faith,* 15–16
Armstrong, Neil, 83
Assemblies of God, **13,** 68, 105–6
Athletes in Action, 123
Athletics, 49–**50,** 57, 71, 121–23
Azusa Street Revival, 14–16

Bakker, Jim, 103–7
Bakker, Tammy Faye, 103–**5**
Baptists, 28, 61, 92–93
Barth, Karl, 41
Beatles, **82–83,** 85
Berlin Wall, 110–11
Bernal, Paul, **117**
Berrigan, Daniel, 84
Berrigan, Philip, 84
Bethel Bible College, 12–13
Birmingham, Alabama, 73

Birth control, 69–70, 89, 97
Black Panther movement, 77
Blanshard, Paul, 64
Bob Jones University, 50, 93–94
Boycotts, 58–59, 70
Branch Davidians, **119**
Brandeis, Louis D., 71
Brandt, John L., 12
*Brown* v. *Board of Education,* 57, 70
Bryan, William Jennings, 25, 29–**30,** 31, 92
Buck, Pearl S., 44
Buddhists, 17–18, 84–85, 114–**15**
Bush, George W., 109, 111
Butler Act, 29–31

Calvary Chapel (Corona del Mar, Calif.), 86–**87**
Campbell, George A., Jr., 11
Canada, 31, 35
Carter, Jimmy, 31, 91–93, 100–**2**
Catholics, 11–12, **19**–20, 39, 47–53, 96–97, **103;** and birth control, 69–70, 89; Charismatic, 68–69; patriotism, **32,** 48–**49;** and political office, 37–38, 63–65, 127; and social reform, 40; and Vatican, 66–67, 69–70; and women's movement, 90; youth, 32–33. *See also* Anti-Catholicism
*Catholic Worker,* 40–**41**
Catholic Youth Organization (CYO), 33, 47
*Challenger* disaster, 113, 128
Charisma, religious, 99–100
Charismatic Renewal movement, 68–69
Cherokee Indians, 18
Chicago, University of, 28
Christian Broadcasting Network (CBN), 102–5, 109

*Christian Century,* 11, 26, 44, 47, 56, 60
Christian Coalition, 109–11
Christian Identity movements, 40, 118–20
Christian Reconstructionism, 110
Church of God in Christ, 68
Church of Jesus Christ of Latter-day Saints. *See* Mormons
Civil rights, 36, 56–**60, 62–63,** 70–81, **88,** 120, 128
Clinton, Bill, 118, 120
Coffin, Henry Sloane, 23, 25
Cold war, 54–55, 110–11
Colorado, University of, 121–**23**
Columbia University, 61
Communism, 40, 45, **49,** 54, 97, 107, 110–11
Concerned Women for America, 101
Congregationalists, 61
Connor, Bull, 73
Conservatives. *See* Evangelicals
Constitutional amendments: First, 19, 110, 118; Eighteenth, 31, 37–38
Coolidge, Calvin, 36
Copeland, Kenneth, 103, 107
Coughlin, Charles E., 39–40
Counterculture, 85–87, 89, 94
Cram, Ralph Adams, 61
*Cross and the Switchblade* (Wilkerson), 68
Cults, 99–100
Cuomo, Mario, 127
Custer, George Armstrong, 18

Dalai Lama, 115
Darrow, Clarence, 29–**30,** 31
Darwin, Charles, 21, 27
Darwinism, 21, 27, 29–31, 40
Day, Dorothy, 40–**41**
"Death of God" theology, 65–66

Dexter Avenue Baptist Church (Montgomery, Ala.), 57–59
Dharmapala, Anagarika, 17
Didion, Joan, 85–86
Dispensationalism, 22–23
Divine, Father, 36–37
Dole, Robert, 109
Doonesbury, **108**
Drew, Timothy, 36
Duquesne University, 67–68

Eisenberg, Sandy, 90
Eisenhower, Dwight D., **42–43,** 61
Ellington, Buford, 71
Episcopalians, 61, 68, **90**
Equal rights amendment (ERA), 90–**91**
Est, 100
Ethical Culture Society, 114
Evangelical Free Church of America, 101
Evangelicals, 13, 21–25, 27, 50–51, 54–55, 86, 92–96, 100–10, 126
Evangelicals for Social Action, 108
Evans, Hiram Wesley, 34
Evening Light Saints, 14
Evers, Medgar, 73
Evolution, theory of. *See* Darwinism; Scopes trial

Falwell, Jerry, 92, 96, 101–2, 103–4
Fard, Wallace D. (Farad Muhammad), 74
Federal Council of Churches, 31–32, **48**
Fellowship of Christian Athletes, 121–23
*Feminine Mystique* (Friedan), 88
Feminist movement, 88, 94, **110**
Focus on the Family, 101
Ford, Gerald, 91
Forman, James, 77, 80

Fosdick, Harry Emerson, 27–28
Frank, Leo, 20–**21**
Free Congress Foundation, 95
Friedan, Betty, 88
Fuller, Charles E., **39**
Fundamentalists, 27–31, 40

Gandhi, Mahatma, 58, 72
Garvey, Marcus, **36,** 74–75
GI Bill of Rights, 48
Gladden, Washington, 23
Glass, Bill, 123
Glossolalia (speaking in tongues), 12–16, 67–68
Goodman, Benny, 71
Grace, Daddy, 36
Grace Chapel Ministries (St. Louis, Mo.), **121**
Graham, Billy, 50–**51,** 54–**55,** 63, **66,** 104, 126
Greek Orthodox Church, 72
Greeley, Andrew, 70
Greeley, Horace, 126
Greenberg, Hank, 71
*Greening of America,* 84

Hahn, Jessica, 104–6
Ham, Mordecai, 50
Hamblen, Stuart, 54
Hare Krishna, 84–85, 114
Harlem Renaissance, 36–37
Harrison, George, **82–83**
Healing, divine, 13–16
Hearst, Patty, 100
Hearst, William Randolph, 54
Hebrew Benevolent Society (Atlanta), 71
Hebrew Union College, 89
Hefley, James C., 123
Hefner, Hugh, 88
Herberg, Will, 45
Heschel, Abraham Joshua, **62–63,** 72
Hindus, 17–18, 84, 114
Hippies. *See* Counterculture
Hirsch, Richard G., **72**

Hocking, William Ernest, 43–44
Holocaust, 44, 46, 65
Homeless persons, 107–**8, 128**
Hoover, Herbert C., 38
*Humanae Vitae,* 69–70, 96

Iakovos, Archbishop, 72
Immigrants, 12, **14**–15, 20–21, 47–48, 60, 114–15
Interchurch Center, **42–43,** 61
Islam. *See* Muslims; Nation of Islam

Jains, 114
Jehovah's Witnesses, 74, 126
"Jesus People," 86–87
Jews, 33–34, 44–47, 65; and civil rights movement, **62–63,** 70–**72;** Orthodox, **125;** Reconstructionist, 90; Reform, 89–90. *See also* Anti-Semitism
John XXIII, Pope, 66–67
John Paul I, Pope, 96–97
Johns, Vernon, 57
Johnson, Lyndon B., **66**
Johnson, Pete, **14**
Johnson, Sonia, 90–**91**
Jones, Jim, 99–100
Jonestown, Guyana, **98**–100
Judeo-Christian tradition, 44–45, 47, 61

Kaplan, Mordecai M., 34
Kennedy, John F., 63–**66,** 73, 80, 110
Kennedy, Robert, 80
King, Martin Luther, Jr., 58–**60,** **62–63,** 72–74, 77, 80–81, 87
Kissinger, Henry, 91
Kit Carson National Forest, New Mexico, 18, 117
Knights of Columbus, **32,** 47
Knights of Mary Phagan, 20
Koresh, David, 119
Krishna, 17
Ku Klux Klan (KKK), 34–**35,** 39–40, 71

Leary, Timothy, 85
Lennon, John, 82–83
Liberals. *See* Modernists
"Liberation theology," 97
Liebman, Joshua, 45
Little Big Horn, Montana, 18
Little Rock, Arkansas, **60**
Los Angeles, California, **14**–16, **38–39**, 54–55
Lutherans, 89

Macfarland, Charles S., 32
Machen, J. Gresham, 28
MacLaine, Shirley, 115
Malcolm X, 75–**79**, 80, 87
Maurin, Peter, 40
McAuliffe, Christa, 113
McCartney, Paul, **82–83**
McCartney, William, 121–24
McPherson, Aimee Semple, **38**–39
McVeigh, Timothy, 119
Meditation, 84–85, **112–13**, 116
Men and religion, 121–24
Mencken, H. L., 30–31
Merton, Thomas, 49–50, **52–53**
Methodist Episcopal Church, 89
Michigan, University of, 68
Michigan State University, 68
Millennium, 125–29
Miller, William, 125–26
Missionaries, 11–16, 18–**19**, 43–44
Modernists, 27–31, 40
Montgomery, Alabama, 57–59
Moody, Dwight L., 22
Moorish Science Temple, 36, 74
Moral Majority, 96
Mormons (Church of Jesus Christ of Latter-day Saints), 13, 90–**91**, 126
Mount Shasta, California, **112–13**, 115–16
Muhammad, Elijah, 74–78
Muslims, 18, 77, **93**, 114–15, **128**. *See also* Nation of Islam

Nakagaki, T. Kenjitsu, **115**
Nation, Carry A., 22
Nation of Islam, 36, 74–80. *See also* Muslims
National Council of Churches, 47–**48**, 51, 60–61, 80
Native Americans, 18–19, 87–**88**, 116–18
Navajo Indians, 18–**19**
Nazis, 44, 46, 118
Neo-Orthodoxy, 41
New Agers, **112–13**, 115–16
New Deal, 38–40
New Mexico, 18–19
Niebuhr, Reinhold, 40–41
*Night* (Wiesel), 46
Nixon, Richard M., 63, 84, 91
Northern Baptist Theological Seminary, 28
Notre Dame, University of, 48–**50**, 68, 127

O'Connell, William H., 11
Oklahoma City bombing, 119–**20**
*Old Fashioned Revival Hour*, **39**
Ordination, 89–**90**
Ozman, Agnes N., **12–13**

Papacy, 11, 66–67, 69–70, 96–97
Parham, Charles Fox, 13–14
Parkhurst, Charles H., 22
Parks, Rosa, 58–**59**
Paul VI, Pope, **69**–70, 96
Peace Mission Movement, 37
Peale, Norman Vincent, 45, 63
Pentecostalism, 12–16
Peoples Temple, **98**–100
Pius X, Pope, 11
*Playboy,* 88, 92
*Plessy* v. *Ferguson,* 57
Pluralism, religious, 44–45, 47, 61, 114–16, 118, 127
Poole, Elijah. *See* Muhammad, Elijah

*Power of Positive Thinking* (Peale), 45
Power Team for Christ, 123
Presbyterians, 28, 61, 89
Presidency, 37–38, 63–**66**, 91–92, 100–2, 106–9
Price, Frederick, 107
Price, Thomas F., 12
Priesand, Sally, 89–90
Promise Keepers, 121–24
Prosperity gospel, 104, 107
Protestantism, mainline, **42–45**, 47–**48**, 60–61. *See also* Judeo–Christian tradition
Pueblo Indians, 18–19, **117**–18

Radio preachers, 38–40, 54–55. *See also* Televangelists
Rauschenbusch, Walter, 23, 58
Reagan, Nancy, 115
Reagan, Ronald, 100–**2**, 106–**8**, 110–11
Reconstructionism, 34
Reed, Ralph, 109
Reformers, social, 21–23, 40, 107–8
Reich, Charles, 84
Religious Right, 45, 92–96, 101, 108–**10**, 127
Religious Roundtable, 101
Revelation, book of, 13, 23, 125–26
Revival preaching, **24–25**, 51, 54–55
Reyna, John C., 19
Richardson, Bobby, 123
Riis, Jacob, 21
Riots, race, 80–**81**
Riverside Church, 61
Roberts, Oral, 105
Robertson, "Pat," 102–4, 108–10
Robinson, Jackie, 57
Robison, James, 103
Rockefeller, John D., Jr., 43
Rockne, Knute, 49
*Roe* v. *Wade,* 94

Roosevelt, Franklin D., 38–40
Rothschild, Jacob, 71
Rubenstein, Richard, 65
Ruby Ridge, Idaho, 119
Ruether, Rosemary Radford, 89
Russell, Charles Taze, 126
Ryan, Leo, 100

St. John the Divine, Cathedral of, 61
St. Luke's Hospital, 61
Salvation Army, 22
Santería, 114
Schneerson, Menachem, **125**
Schools: Catholic, 33, 48–50; Christian, 95; Native American, **19**; prayer in, 96, 108; public, 29–30, 65
Schuller, Robert, 103
Scientology, 100
Scopes, John, T., 29–31
Scopes trial, 29–31, 65, 92, 95
Scoville Tabernacle, **10–11**
Scudder, John, 122–23
Sedona, Arizona, 116
*Seven Storey Mountain* (Merton), 49–50, 52–53
Sexual revolution, 88–89
Seymour, William J., 14
Sheen, Fulton J., 45
Sheldon, Charles, 122
Shiel, Bernard J., 33
Sider, Ronald, 108
Sikhs, 84, 114
Simmons, William J., 34
Sioux Indians, 18, 87–**88**
Sit-ins, 70–**71**
Sitting Bull, **88**
Slaton, John, 20
Smith, Alfred E., 37–38
Smith, Chuck, 86–**87**
Smith, Joseph, 126
Social Gospel, 23, 25–26, 58
Sojourners, 108
Soup kitchens, 107–**8**

Southern Baptists, 92–94
Southern Christian Leadership Conference (SCLC), 59
"Spiritual gifts," 67–69
*Sputnik*, 65
Starr, Ringo, **82–83**
Stewart, Lyman and Milton, 27
Sunday, Billy, **24–25**, 122
Sun Myung Moon, 100
Supreme Court, U.S., 57, 59, 71, 94, 118
Swaggart, Jimmy, 103–**6**
Symbionese Liberation Army, 100
Synagogue Council of America, 33–34

Taoism, 84
Taos, NM, 18–19, 116–18
Televangelists, 54–55, 96, 101–7. *See also* Radio preachers
Templeton, Charles, **51**, 54
Terrorism, 114–15, 119–21
Terry, Randall, 109
Tilton, Robert, 107
Traditional Values Coalition, 96, 101
Transcendental Meditation, 84–85
Trappists, 49, 52–53
Truman, Harry, 57
Tuskegee Institute, 56

Unification Church, 100
Union of American Hebrew Congregations, 72
Union Theological Seminary, 25, 40, 61
United Church of Canada, 31
United Methodist Church, 89
Universal Negro Improvement Association, **36**, 74

Vatican II, 66–67, 69, 96
Vedantism, 17
Vietnam War, 40, 80, 83–84, 91

Vivekananda, Swami, **17**
Vodou, 114

Waco, Texas, **119**
Wallis, Jim, 108
Walsh, James A., 12
Washington, Booker T., 56
Watergate scandal, 91
Watson, Tom, 20
Watts, Alan, 84–**85**
Weaver, Randy, 119
Webb, Mohammed, 18
Westminister Theological Seminary, 28
Weyrich, Paul, 94–95
White supremacists, 40, 56, 71, 118–19
Wickersham, Dave, 123
Wiesel, Elie, **46**
Wilkerson, David, 68
Wilson, Woodrow, 25, 71
Winrod, Gerald Burton, 40
Women's movement, 88–**91**, 94, **110**
Woodstock Music Festival, 83
World's Fairs, 44, **50**, 65, 83, 113
World's Parliament of Religions, 17–18
World War I, 25–27, 32, 37, 40–41
World War II, 44–46, 48
Worthington, Al, 123
Wounded Knee, SD, 87, 118

Xenolalia, 15

Y2K computer bug, 128
Yogi, Mahesh, **82–83**, 85
Young, Brigham, 13
Young Men's Christian Association (YMCA), 22, 32–33
Young Women's Christian Association (YWCA), 22, 33
Youth for Christ, 51

Zen Buddhism, 84–85

# Acknowledgments

My greatest inspiration, as always, is my family. It is my fondest (though perhaps forlorn) hope that Christian, Andrew, and Sara—all of them teenagers—might find something of interest in these pages. My life would be impoverished to the point of hopelessness without the love, humor, and companionship of Catharine, my wife.

I gratefully acknowledge the expert assistance of my friends Harry Stout and Jon Butler, the general editors of this series, and all of the production people at Oxford University Press, who have conspired to produce this handsome volume. Nancy Toff at Oxford is a meticulous and demanding reader, which makes her a superb editor. Thank you.

Writing a book intended for younger readers provides a welcome occasion to acknowledge the students and teachers who shaped me at East Chain Consolidated School in rural southern Minnesota, Wenona Elementary School and Kolb Junior High School in Bay City, Michigan, and Meredith Junior High School and Hoover High School in Des Moines, Iowa. I am proud to be a product of public education, which I believe stands alongside baseball, jazz music, and the First Amendment as America's noblest contributions to Western civilization. Despite a legion of critics, public schools, I am convinced, remain our best hope for the survival of American democracy.

And yes, Mr. Grein, wherever you may be, I can still recite "Stopping by Woods on a Snowy Evening" from start to finish.

# Picture Credits

Photo by David Allen: 120; Archive Photos: 82 (Express Newspapers/L–166/), 119 (Reuters/G. Reed); Archives of the Billy Graham Center, Wheaton, IL: 55, 66; Copyright Dan Budnik/Woodfin Camp: 117; ©Roger Ressmeyer/CORBIS: 112; DOONESBURY ©1984 G.B. Trudeau. Reprinted with permission of UNIVERSAL PRESS SYNDICATE. All rights reserved: 108; Courtesy of The Archives of the Episcopal Church USA: 90; Florida State Archives: 110; Flower Pentecostal Heritage Center: 13, 38, 105, 106; The Franciscan Friars of the St. Barbara Province: 19; Courtesy of Fuller Theological Seminary, Pasadena, CA: 39; Special Collections, J. Willard Marriott Library, University of Utah: 91; The Jacob Rader Marcus Center of the American Jewish Archives: 21, 46, 62,72, 125; Courtesy John F. Kennedy Library (Pre-Presidential Papers, Box 1017): 64; Courtesy Liberty University: 102; Library of Congress: 2 (NYWTS), 10 (LC-USZ62-63886), 24 (LC-USZ62-84387), 30 (LC-USZ62-114986), 32–33 (Pan Subject—Groups, no.159 (E size)), 36 (LC-USZ62-109628), 49 (LC-219710), 52 (NYWTS), 59 (LC-USZ62-109643), 69 (LC-USZ62-114652), 71 (NYWTS), 79 (LC-USZ62-11169), 88 (LC-USZ62-127427); Marquette University Archives: 41; Frederick Detwiller, *Temples of God and Gold,* ©Museum of the City of New York: cover; National Archives: 35 (306-NT-650-11), 60 (306-PSC-63-4119), 75 (412-DA-13792), 76, 81 (362-VS-3F-5999-13), 93 (412-DA-13061), 98 (342-B-ND-064-12-115541); Photo by Rose Johnson-Mackey/Courtesy of the National Coalition for Burned Churches: 121; National Council of Churches: 42, 48; New York Buddhist Church: 115; Presbyterian Historical Society, Presbyterian Church (U.S.A.) (Philadelphia): 6; Religion News Service: 123; Seaver Center for Western History Research, Los Angeles County Museum of Natural History: 14; Photo by Brother Placid Stuckenschneider O.S.B., Saint John's Abbey: 103; Courtesy of Charles Templeton: 51; Julian Wasser/TimePix: 87; Photo Courtesy of University of Notre Dame Archives: 50; Courtesy of the Vedanta Society of St. Louis, 205 S. Skinker Blvd., St. Louis, MO 63105: 17; Courtesy Richard Wormser: 128.

# Text Credits

"The Azusa Street Revival in Los Angeles," p.16: *Apostolic Faith,* September 1906, p.1.

"The Evils of War," p.26: *Christian Century,* December 27, 1917.

"The Holocaust Nightmare," p.46: Elie Wiesel, *Night* (New York: Hill & Wang, 1960), p.44.

"An American Monk," pp. 52–53: Thomas Merton, *The Seven Storey Mountain* (New York: Harcourt, Brace & World, 1948), pp. 382–88, 396–405.

"A Black Man's Conversion," pp. 78–79: Malcolm X, with Alex Haley, *The Autobiography of Malcolm X* (New York: Random House, 1964), pp. 163–64.

"The Origins of the Religious Right," p.95: Michael Cromartie, ed., *No Longer Exiles: The Religious New Right in American Politics* (Washington, D.C.: Ethics and Public Policy Center, 1993), pp. 25–26.

"Pueblos Make Their Case for Taos Blue Lake," p.117: *Congressional Record,* 91st Congress, 2nd Session.

"Religion in a Pluralistic Society," p.127: Mario M. Cuomo, "Religious Belief and Public Morality," *New York Review of Books,* October 25, 1984, p.32.

## Randall Balmer

Randall Balmer is the Ann Whitney Olin Professor of American Religion at Barnard College, Columbia University. His commentaries and op-ed pieces have appeared in newspapers throughout the United States, including the *Des Moines Register*, *New York Newsday*, the *St. Louis Post–Dispatch*, and the *New York Times*. He has received numerous awards, for both journalistic and scholarly writing. PBS turned Balmer's 1989 volume *Mine Eyes Have Seen the Glory: A Journey into the Evangelical Subculture in America* into an award-winning television series, for which he received an Emmy nomination as writer and host.

## Jon Butler

Jon Butler is the William Robertson Coe Professor of American Studies and History and Professor of Religious Studies at Yale University. He received his B.A. and Ph.D. in history from the University of Minnesota. He is the coauthor, with Harry S. Stout, of *Religion in American History: A Reader*, and the author of several other books in American religious history including *Awash in a Sea of Faith: Christianizing the American People*, which won the Beveridge Award for the best book in American history in 1990 from the American Historical Association.

## Harry S. Stout

Harry S. Stout is the Jonathan Edwards Professor of American Christianity at Yale University. He is the general editor of the Religion in America series for Oxford University Press and co-editor of *Readings in American Religious History*, *New Directions in American Religious History*, *A Jonathan Edwards Reader*, and *The Dictionary of Christianity in America*. His book *The Divine Dramatist: George Whitefield and the Rise of Modern Evangelicalism* was nominated for a Pulitzer Prize in 1991.